Praise for Michael E. Gerber, Russell O'Connell, and *The E-Myth Home Cleaning Business*

There are a great many striking things about Russell O'Connell—his contagious energy, drive and attention to detail aren't lost on anyone. But what makes him unique to me is his ability to employ first-principles thinking, identifying patterns and systemising business in completely new, innovative ways. Merging a deep understanding of how people work with the latest technology, he tailors processes that are as intuitive as they are efficient and profitable.

Russell possesses exceptional insights across entrepreneurialism, systems-based thinking and digital innovation. He's also very good at making his knowledge accessible. Talking to Russell, you start seeing things in a different light—where there were seemingly unsurmountable challenges, there are suddenly boundless opportunities.

I can think of no one else to better CoAuthor a book with Michael E. Gerber. And, indeed, I'm sure you'll enjoy reading this as much as I did.

Peter Barclay, Business Development Manager, SixSix

Russell's mind is a circus tent for ideas, overflowing with acro batic logic and unicycle-riding solutions. Working with him isn't like running a linear project where you simply overcome the immediately obvious challenges. Russell finds completely different ways of looking at things, bulldozing norms and replacing them with ground-breaking new standards. You find yourself thinking, "why on Earth hasn't this always been done THIS way instead—it makes perfect sense!"

Driven by a rocket-pack innovative spirit, Russell is at the very frontier of business development, leaving the status quo discarded in his dust. This guy is the leading act in any endeavour he takes on—a true ringmaster of success!

Alex Morrison, Director, Integral Media

As a franchise marketing specialist, I've had the privilege of consulting with visionary CEOs across the globe. Russell O'Connell, however, stands out for his ability to integrate technology and systems for business scalability.

Witnessing his journey has been nothing short of awe-inspiring. He has literally revolutionised the field of residential cleaning services. Russell hasn't only developed and extraordinary business, but by embracing cutting-edge technology, he has crafted a unique and powerful advantage for MyHome – a case study of disruptive innovation.

Really, MyHome partners aren't so much running a home-cleaning company as they are owners of a digital business that just happens to be in the residential services industry. This attracts a completely different calibre of franchise partners – high quality business owners with great people and management skills who will break barriers to provide the very best service. And the MyHome customers are naturally all the much better for it! Russell matches his strategic and tactical brilliance with a captivating personality and social skills.

Frank Tzimas, Founder, GrowthHive Franchise Marketing

I've had the pleasure of working closely with Russell in developing a proprietary app, MyOP, for MyHome. During this time, I've seen first-hand his ability to systemise operations by integrating cutting-edge digital systems and AI—effectively transforming MyHome and setting completely new standards for the home-cleaning industry. His hands-on approach during the design and testing of the MyOP system ensured its alignment with the practical needs of the business, reflecting his desire to systemise and attain operational excellence.

Beyond his professional expertise, Russell's energy and drive are contagious. Russell has an excellent ability to communicate and align teams toward a common, clearly expressed goal. The transformation he has driven within the residential services sector, through systematic and AI-enhanced processes has set a new benchmark for efficiency and ease of operation encapsulating the essence of a 'business in a box' model.

Anthony Sapountzis, CTO & Co-founder, Aerion Technologies

My first memory of Russell and MyHome is from walking into an immaculate office, where everything was strategicall placed. There was even a "Welcoming Aerion Technologies" sign in the foyer—a detail I had never seen before during my 15 years in business.

This would come as no surprise to anyone who knows Russell. He leaves and breathes systemisation and process, and he has a keen eye for detail. He's also a people person, so being thoughtful and understanding is second nature to him.

I know that he's accomplished a great lot during his life as an entrepreneur, but he still has that openness to new ideas, he still maintains that beginner's mind that Michael E. Gerber talks about. Maybe that's how I first and foremost think of Russell O'Connell, from whom I've learnt so much—he is always, always looking for ways to improve.

Andrew Romeo, CEO & Co-founder, Aerion Technologies

Russell O'Connell is a true visionary and master business practitioner. His ability to create and implement incredible systems and processes that consistently deliver outstanding (and repeatable) results is unique. His talent for being able to make an ordinary business extraordinary is unmatched.

By embracing and mastering The E-Myth methodology, and harnessing some of the most powerful digital, automation and AI business tools available, Russell shows how Michael E. Gerber's E-Myth is more relevant and accessible than ever in today's digital age.

Read this book and learn from two true masters—Michael E. Gerber and Russell O'Connell. One, the pioneer of the methodology that has transformed countless small businesses around the globe, the other a master of real-world, day-to-day, technology-driven application. An incredibly potent combination. Your business—and your life—will be so much the better for reading and learning from these two great minds.

Haydn Rowe, Managing Director, Results Corporation

Michael E. Gerber's The E-Myth is one of only four books I recommend As required reading. For those looking to start and build a business of their wn, this is the man who has coached more successful entrepreneurs than the next ten gurus combined.

Timothy Ferris, #1 New York Times best-selling author, The 4-Hour Workweek

Michael's understanding of entrepreneurship and small-business management has been a difference maker for countless businesses, including Infusion Software. His insights into the entrepreneurial process of building a business are a must-read for every small-business owner. The vision, clarity, and leadership that came out of our Dreaming RoomTM experience were just what our company needed to recognize our potential and motivate the whole company to achieve it.

Clate Mask, president and CEO, Infusion Software

Everyone needs a mentor, someone who tells it like it is, holds you accountable, and shows you your good, bad, and ugly. For millions

of small-business owners, Michael E. Gerber is that person. Let Michael be your mentor and you are in for a kick in the pants, the ride of a lifetime.

John Jantsch, author, Duct Tape Marketing

Michael E. Gerber's strategies in The E-Myth were instrumental in building my company from two employees to a global organization; I can't wait to see how applying the strategies from Awakening the Entrepreneur Within will affect its growth!

Dr. Ivan Misner, founder and chairman, BNI; author, Masters of Sales

Because of Michael E. Gerber, I transformed my twenty-four-hour-a-day, seven-day-a-week job (also called a small business) into a multimillion-dollar turnkey business. This in turn set the foundation for my worldwide training firm. I am living my dream because of Michael E. Gerber.

Howard Partridge, Phenomenal Products Inc.

Michael E. Gerber is a truly remarkable man. His steady openness of Mind and ability to get to the deeper level continue to be an inspiration and encouragement to me. He seems to always ask that one question that orces the new perspective to break open, and he approaches the new coming method in a fearless way.

Rabbi Levi Cunin, Chabad of Malibu

Michael E. Gerber is an incredible business philosopher, guru, perhaps even a seer. He has an amazing intuition, which allows him to see in an instant what everybody else is missing; he sees opportunity everywhere. While I was in the Dreaming RoomTM, Michael gave me the gift of seeing through the eyes of an awakened entrepreneur, and instantly my business changed from a regional success to serving clients on four continents.

Keith G. Schiehl, president, Rent-a-Geek Computer Services

Michael E. Gerber forced me to think big, think real, and gave me the support network to make it happen. A new wave of entrepreneurs is rising, much in thanks to his amazing efforts and very practical approach to doing business. Michael E. Gerber is among the very few who truly understand entrepreneurship and small business. While others talk about these topics in the form of theories, methodologies, processes, and so on, Michael goes to the heart of the issues. Whenever Michael writes about entrepreneurship, soak it in, as it is not only good for your business, but great for your soul. His words will help you to keep your passion and balance while sailing through the uncertain sea of entrepreneurship.

Raymond Yeh, CoAuthor, The Art of Business

Trinity Property Investments Inc., Home Vestors franchises I thought E-Myth was an awkward name! What could this book do for me? But when I finally got to reading it... it was what I was looking for all along. Then, to top it off, I took a twenty-seven-hour trip to San Diego just to attend the Dreaming RoomTM, where Michael touched my heart, my mind, and my soul.

Helmi Natto, president, Eye 2 Eye Optics, Saudi Arabia

I went to the Dreaming RoomTM to have Michael E. Gerber fix my business. He talked about Dreaming. What was this Dreaming? I was too busy working! Too busy being miserable, angry, frustrated, behind in what I was trying to accomplish. And losing everything I was working for. Then Michael E. Gerber woke up the dreamer in me and remade my life and my business.

Pat Doorn, president, Mountain View Electric Ltd.

Michael E. Gerber's gift to isolate the issues and present simple, direct, business-changing solutions shines bright with Awakening the Entrepreneur Within. If you're interested in developing an entrepreneurial vision and plan that inspires others to action, buy this book, read it, and apply the processes Gerber brilliantly defines

Tim Templeton, author, The Referral of a Lifetime

The Dreaming Room™ experience was literally life-changing for us. Within months, we were able to start our foundation and make several television appearances owing to his teachings. He has an incredible charisma, which is priceless, but above all Michael E. Gerber awakens passion from within, enabling you to take action with dramatic results... starting today!

Shona and Shaun Carcary

The E Myth Home Cleaning Business

Why Most Home Cleaning Companies Don't Work and What to Do About It

MICHAEL E. GERBER
RUSSELL O'CONNELL

PRODIGY
BUSINESS BOOKS

Published by
Prodigy Business Books, Inc.

Production Team
Michael E. Gerber, Author, Michael E. Gerber Companies Inc; Russell O'connell, CoAuthor, MyHome® Australia; Prodigy Business Books, Inc, Book Production, Michael E.Gerber Companies Inc.; Amethyst Rosenauer, Book Division Manager, Michael E.Gerber Companies Inc.; Chris Groote, Editor; Erich Broesel, Cover Designer, Brosel Design, Inc.; Jeff Kassebaum, Author photographe , Jeff Kassebaum and Co

For general information on other products and services, please visit the website: www.michaelegerbercompanies.com.

ISBN 978-1-61835-016-9 (hbk)
ISBN 979-8-350974-84-3 (ebk)

Printed in the United States of America

To Luz Delia, whose heart expands mine,
whose soul inspires mine,
Whose boldness reaches for the stars, thank you,
forever, for being, truly mine...

—Michael E Gerber

To my wife Sara,
Your spirit flows with the grace of tai chi
bringing harmony and strength to my life.
This is for you, my guiding light and endless inspiration.

—Russell O'Connell

CONTENTS

A WORD ABOUT THIS BOOK

Michael E. Gerber

My first E-Myth book was published in 1985. It was the beginning of a long and enthralling exercise, called, by me, waking everyone up!

I named it, *The E-Myth: Why Most Businesses Don't Work and What to Do About It.*

The term, *E-Myth*, stood for the entrepreneurial myth. The fact that most small business owners aren't truly the entrepreneurs everyone thinks they are, but what I came to call, "technicians suffering from an entrepreneurial seizure!

Since that book, and the company I created to provide business development services to its many readers, millions have read *The E-Myth* and the books that followed it, starting out with *The E-Myth Revisited*, and continuing with the more than 30 books which followed on its heels, along with the tens upon tens of thousands of small business owners who have participated in our E-Myth Mastery programs.

Since *The E-Myth Revisited* took the marketplace by storm, it became obvious to me that there was needed another series of books which addressed the application of my E-Myth Protocol in an entire subset of small companies, each of whom have been attracted to *The E-Myth* and applied its thinking to the extreme development of their uniquely designed Practices. The Practice of Law, or Chiropractic, of Landscape

Contracting, et al. There are now twenty-two of those "vertical books" addressing the seemingly unique problems of every field of endeavor, only to discover that my E-Myth Protocol has been applied successfully, and systematically, to each and every one of them.

So, my CoAuthors have become the most avid fans of our work, having told the story of how it has worked to grow their companies to a degree never thought possible before.

That's when the idea for this book series came about. What I think of as the Core Operating Series, CoAuthored by experts in each of the most critical strategic functions needing to be filled in every small growing compan .

I think of those Strategic Functions as Financial, Legal, Operational, Strategic Leadership, Marketing, Technological, Social, and Administrative.

Think CFO, CEO, COO, CIO, CTO, CMO, CLO, and CAO.

In short, think of getting one's house in order across the broad expanse of the Strategic Reach of any company as it grows from tiny to transformational.

It is our position that to be inordinately successful, every small company owner needs to assume the responsibility for each of these Eight Strategic Roles, until such time as he or she is able to replace him or herself with the individuals designated to fill those roles

Since there's no better way of accomplishing an objective than by simply getting started with it, let's get started.

Allow me to introduce you to Russell O'Connell, a brilliant entrepreneur from Australia, who is committed to E-Myth Systems and creating profitable and replicable business, which happens to be a remarkable home cleaning business .

Welcome to *The E-Myth Home Cleaning Business!*

What a brilliant opportunity for each of us to grow exponentially and to understand how that works.

—Michael E. Gerber

CoFounder, Chairman

Michael E. Gerber Companies, Inc. Katy,

Texas

www.michaelegerbercompanies.com

A NOTE FROM RUSSELL

In the mid noughties I had the big house , the trips to Europe, the Aston Martin , more money than I could possible need ...... the whole package .

Yet only a couple of years later, I choose to step down as business leader and leave it all behind .

Why?

Well to get to that we need to start at the beginning.

In my early days, I was a doer. A hard worker. A go-getter.

I was an entrepreneur, too—in the sense that I started and ran successful businesses in real estate, fashion, cosmetics, and hospitality.

I spent countless years working *in* these businesses.

But it was only after I had attended a talk by Michael E. Gerber and read his book, The E-Myth, that I saw the blueprint for how to work on your business to create a business that works for you. A business that you can separate from yourself, scale indefinitely—and when you are ready, exit your business at a high value multiple.

Michael turned me on to the power of systems, and I've never looked back. From that day on I became a 'systems guy' This approach, to me, is true entrepreneurship.

Now, since you're reading this book, I'm pretty sure that you're also a high-achieving doer. And you have my deepest respect for that. Grit and discipline are certainly required to succeed with anything in life. But there's also this: if you spend all your time doing, doing, doing, you'll never be able to scale your business—and you'll never be free from work, worry and the relentless treadmill.

That's what happens to the vast majority of home-cleaning businesses. It's such an easy market to get into that it attracts doers who think they will be able to work themselves to the top. That never happens, though. You don't work yourself to wealth. You create wealth by innovating and standardizing systems for others to work to.

The good news is that you've picked a great industry. Really, take heart. As an experienced entrepreneur, I have been in the privileged position to be able to select pretty much any market I fancied for my next venture. And I CHOSE home-cleaning. It was a carefully considered, deliberate choice. Not because I have any particular interest in cleaning, but because home-cleaning services offer an unbeatable opportunity to apply systems-based thinking. And as you'll discover, I passionately believe that true business success is intrinsically linked to systems.

Most home-cleaning businesses just sell a service, to anyone who will buy, usually on an hourly rate—and usually, it's the owner of the business doing the cleaning.

As a systems-based entrepreneur, you will be one of the few exceptions to this rule. You will put a high value on your own time, and so, you will be selling your teams' time—the technicians who execute on YOUR plans—to people who consider their time worth a lot. What's more, you will leverage digital tools to automate much of the processes around this work.

As you will see, everyone—your customers, employees, and suppliers—wins.

This book will tell you how. And there will be nothing standing in your way to success.

I'd wish you good luck, but you won't need it. Indeed, that's much of the point of this book. Take ownership of the advice, and you will be able to predict your success with mathematical precision.

What you'll find throughout these pages constitutes the very soul of every truly successful business.

Study it.

Master it.

Use it to write your own success story.

—Russell O'Connell
Founder/CEO
MyHome
Melbourne, Australia
www.myhomefranchise.com.au

PREFACE

Michael E. Gerber

Over the past four decades, it's been my delight to inspire small business owners in every trade and profession to acquire and to apply the methods and skills we've invented and perfected for the purpose of growing and thriving in their role as entrepreneurs.

Most important in our work has been the Dream, Vision, Purpose and Mission that resides at the heart of it, without which nothing we've accomplished for the millions of small business owners we've reached out to and touched would have, could have, made any difference

So too has that unadulterated passion been the source for many of the ways I've taught and shared premises of The E-Myth, from the scores of Dreaming Rooms I led for nearly twenty years, to the online programs we built, such as Radical U, to the thousands of business owners I've coached one on one.

As you, the owner of a home cleaning business, read Russell's story, and the absolutely profound success he's created utilizing my E-Myth Philosophy, Paradigm and Tools, know that at the foundation of it all is the entrepreneurial energy and imagination that lies within this book, and within you, right now.

Welcome to the extraordinary world of INSPIRATION.

Welcome to the first day of the rest of your life

Michael E. Gerber
Chief Dreamer
CoFounder/Chairman Michael
E. Gerber Companies
Radical U
Prodigy Business Books
The Dreaming Room

ACKNOWLEDGMENTS

Michael E. Gerber

As always, and never to be forgotten, there are those who give of themselves to make my work possible.

To my dearest and most forgiving partner, wife, friend, and CoFounder, Luz Delia Gerber, whose love and commitment takes me to places I would often not go unaccompanied.

Chris Groote, who so freely gives of his time and expertise, and has seemingly never said no to any task I've asked. To Erich Broesel, our stand-alone graphic designer and otherwise visual genius who supported the creation of all things visual that will forever be all things Gerber, we thank you, deeply, for your continuous contribution of things both temporal and eternal.

To Johanna Nilsson, who told us that social media was much, much more than just social, and then, with the grace G-d gave her, and proved it every step of the way.

To those many, many dreamers, thinkers, storytellers, and leaders, whose travels with me in The Dreaming Room have given me life, breath, and pleasure unanticipated before we met. To those many participants in my life (you know who you are), thank you for taking me seriously, and joining me in this exhilarating quest.

And, of course, to my CoAuthors, all of you, your genius, wisdom, intelligence, and wit have supplied me with a grand view of the world, which would never have been the same without you.

Love to all.

ACKNOWLEDGMENTS

Russell O'Connell

It's like Michael says—every business is a family business. And that, to me, includes everyone who is touched by what we do. Starting, of course, with my own family.

To my loving wife, Sara. You've taught me the true meaning of success—about the things that really matter in life. We've been married for over 30 years, and you've supported me 100% through all the ups and downs. No tribute can do you justice. I'm a truly lucky man to have you in my life.

And to our wonderful daughter, Shen Lin. You've always taught me so much about myself—you make me want to be the best version of Russell that I can be, and I'm incredibly proud of you in every way.

This book is dedicated to Roy Grundy, my late, great mate. Without you, Roy, I would never have had half the adventures and fun that I've enjoyed, and I might have spent my whole life trying to figure out what you taught me in such a short time. To this day, I still find myself asking, "What would Roy do here? What would Roy think about this?" It's like you're still here guiding me now. You were my mentor and best friend—and now I have the greatest memories and amazing stories to tell.

To Haydn Rowe and the team at Results Corporation in the UK: you haven't only helped develop MyHome since 2002—you've been and continue to be the guardians of our brand. From logos, taglines and web through to graphics, brochures and magazines, you've played an integral part. My heartfelt thanks for it all!

To Jon Pither and Bruce Rowan, who are no longer with us, deserve special acknowledgement. Jon, as my first chairperson, you brought invaluable business and governance experience, and you were always willing to provide a guiding hand. And, Bruce, as my first investor, you were happy to back me financially whenever I needed it. Together with Jon, you steered me through the complex labyrinth required for listing a public company. I'm deeply grateful to have had you both at my side.

To my accountant, Arif Virani—no ordinary bean counter—you're a fellow entrepreneur with numerous business interests of your own. A true inspiration! You've helped me not only to understand the meaning behind the numbers, and what prudent actions to take when I needed advice. I've always enjoyed our annual meetings in Dubai and repeatedly find myself looking for excuses to come visit. Looking forward to the next one!

My heartfelt thanks to my fellow director, Martin Coyle: it's a genuine pleasure to have you on the board. I still remember how we met at that industry show in Ireland over 20 years ago—I heard your Aussie accent and we became instant friends! You're a true renaissance man, an invaluable counterbalance and a fantastic sounding board.

To the team at our head offic in Melbourne - past and present: Simon Holms, my right-hand man for the past eight years—master of discipline, strong, dependable and always in my corner; Katharine and Georgia—we braved some tough times together during the pandemic, and I've so enjoyed seeing you both grow from enthusiastic novices into accomplished team members and confident young ladies as well; Mark

Piggot—a truly decent man and friend , Farhan (you know why) and Adeel Shiek, you've been my numbers guy in Australia for over nine years now—and for good reason, thank you!

There is a special group of people in the UK who played a crucial role in the development of MyHome in the noughties. There are too many to mention, but I will forever be grateful to Dee, my hugely capable PA, and Tamarin, our wonderful designer and master of getting things done, as well as a wider group of talented people including Robert Dancy, Richard and Renee, Robert Boot, Johnathon and Simon, Neal Gossage and Tony Hoskinson who played key roles in growing and supporting our fast-growing franchise network and listed business.

Thanks also go to Anthony and Andrew and the team at Aerion Technologies for helping capture our systematic approach to business and aiding with our digital transformation. It's been a fun journey, and our beautiful IT platform, MyOP™, is making life easier for the entire MyHome community of staff, customers, and franchise partners. Working with you gives us confidence that we can fulfil our vision of being a high-tech, high-touch organization, and we're truly excited about taking on the future possibilities of AI—and beyond—with you!

Finally, to Josie Kelly. What can I say!? My favorite franchise partner, you've taken what was already so great about MyHome and made it so much greater. You showed me how MyHome could be a business that delivers a great income AND a great lifestyle. That it could be something more valuable than "just a profitable franchise". You are now our brand advocate avatar and poster girl! You've made MyHome your home and you use it to enrich your own life and those of everyone around you. Well, that's quite something. I love your quick wit and quirky sense of humor that we share. You are an inspiration and a marvelous friend.

To all of you mentioned here, and to the numerous other people I've had the pleasure of sharing my life with—thank you!

Everything we do, we ultimately do for each other.

You all literally mean the world to me.

INTRODUCTION

Michael E. Gerber

As I write this book, the marketplace continues to do what it has always done; it goes up and it goes down. Today, in 2024, it's terrifyingly skittish.

Inflation, global threats, political turmoil; it could tear your heart out, or it could make you incredibly wealthy.

What has always been true, however, is that the marketplace lives by rules great companies don't.

The marketplace is an emotional storm, where rules one day defy attitudes the very next.

Where the truth on Monday is beset upon by the truth like a ferocious dog on Tuesday.

If one were to run a company like the marketplace runs, disaster would be the common experience.

Come to think of it, while great companies do exactly the opposite of what the marketplace does, most companies unfortunately aren't great companies.

And that's why the vast majority of small companies which start up in any one year almost equal the number of small companies which close their doors in those very same years.

Think about it: for every one hundred new companies started, half of them fail in that very same year!

Doesn't matter what kind of company it is, either.

When a company, small or large, is operated based upon emotional decisions, that company is doomed to fail. And, from the very beginning to the very end, the vast majority of small companies are purely operated by emotional decisions, choices, preferences, opinions, attitudes, beliefs, and hopes.

Thus, this book.

CHAPTER

1

The Story of Steve and Peggy

Michael E. Gerber

"You leave home to seek your fortune and, when you get it, you go home and share it with your family."

—Anita Baker

Every business is a family business. To ignore this truth is to court disaster.

I don't care if family members actually work in the business or not. Whatever his or her relationship with the business, every member of a home cleaning business owner's family will be greatly affected by the decisions that business owner makes about the business. There's just no way around it.

Unfortunately, like most small business owners, those in the home cleaning industry tend to compartmentalize their lives. They view their business as a *job* - what they do - and therefore none of their family's business.

"This has nothing to do with you," says the owner to his wife, with blind conviction. "I leave work at the offic and family at home."

And with equal conviction, I say, "Not true!"

In actuality, your family and contracting business are inextricably linked to one another. What's happening in your business is also happening at home. Consider the following and ask yourself if each is true:

- If you're angry at work, you're also angry at home.
- If you're out of control in your home cleaning business, you're equally out of control at home.
- If you're having trouble with money in your company, you're also having trouble with money at home.
- If you have communication problems in your business, you're also having communication problems at home.
- If you don't trust in your company, you don't trust at home.
- If you're secretive in your business, you're equally secretive at home.

And you're paying a huge price for it!

The truth is that your business and your family are one - and you're the link. Or you should be. Because if you try to keep your business and your family apart, if your business and your family are strangers, you will effectively create two separate worlds that can never wholeheartedly serve each other. Two worlds that split each other apart.

Let me tell you the story of Steve and Peggy Walsh.

The Walshes met when they were both in college. They were lab partners in Chemistry 102, Steve fulfilling the minimal science requirements his Business Administration degree would require, and Peggy was working towards her Bachelor's in Sociology. When their lab discussions started to wander beyond reagents and solvents into their personal lives, they discovered they had a lot in common. By the end of the course, they weren't just talking in class; they were talking on the phone every night ... and *not* about chemical equations.

Steve thought Peggy was absolutely brilliant (her love for dogs was astounding), and Peggy considered Steve the most passionate man she knew. It wasn't long before they were engaged and planning their future together. A week after graduation, they were married in a lovely garden ceremony in Peggy's childhood home.

While Steve landed a low-level management position with a successful regional corporation, Peggy continued school, working towards her Masters and working part time for a local non-profit. Over the next few years, the couple worked hard to keep their finances afloat. They worked long hours, Steve climbing the ladder in his company while Peggy continued to work and study; they were often exhausted and struggled to make ends meet. But throughout it all, they were committed to what they were doing and to each other.

Even though Steve had a knack for numbers and people, it seemed as though he was always being missed for promotion. At the same time, Peggy completed her studies, but struggled to find a career path that would reward her for her education, so she continued to work for the non-profit. Not long after, Steve found a middle management position with a large, publicly traded commercial property management group. Less than two years later, the couple had their first son, and Peggy decided to take some time off from the non-profit to be with him. Those were good years. Steve and Peggy loved each other very much, were active members in their church, participated in community organizations, and spent quality time together. The Walshes considered themselves one of the most fortunate families they knew, even if money was tight from time to time.

But work became troublesome. Steve grew increasingly frustrated with the way the company was run, the travel it often required of him, the feeling he wasn't being paid what he was worth, and the hectic schedules that sometimes kept him in the offic until after nine o'clock at night. "I want to be in control of my own destiny," he announced one night at the dinner table. "I want to find something I can do that pays well and doesn't require so much time."

Steve and Peggy spent many nights talking about the idea. Was it something they could afford? Did Steve really have the skills necessary to open up a business? What industry could he even break into? At the same time, Peggy admitted she wanted to get back into the workforce, and she pointed out a close friend cleaned homes and seemed to always be busy.

With that, Steve began to think about what home cleaning actually meant. He knew there couldn't really be much to it - simply clean what was dirty, right? He'd always kept his home clean, even when he was single, and while Peggy was pregnant, and even after the baby was born, he'd taken on the majority of the housecleaning duties until Peggy had been physically well enough to handle it. He began to think about what makes a home cleaning business a success? Were there enough customers to go around? What impact would such a move have on their lives, their lifestyle, their son, their relationship? They asked all the questions they thought they needed to answer before Steve went into business for himself ... but they never really drew up a concrete plan.

While all this was going on, Steve's company went through a series of layoffs and downsizing due to a slowdown in the economy. While he was surprised he'd lost his job, Steve took it as a sign his idea of a home cleaning company was on the right track, and he secretly welcomed the idea of the freedom he now had to control his own destiny.

Steve committed to starting his own home cleaning company. Peggy, despite her worries, agreed it was surely a perfect opportunity - they'd been talking about it for months, and this was certainly the push they needed. Peggy happily offered her own commitment to help in any way she could. So, Steve made up a logo, got the necessary business licenses filed, took some money from their retirement accounts, and began placing ads and fliers around the town

In the beginning, things went well. A housing boom had hit the town, and new families were pouring into the area. Steve had no trouble getting new customers. His business expanded, quickly outpacing his schedule.

At the same time, he'd found there was no trouble fin - ing employees to help with the work, and within a matter of months, Steve had three people he'd subcontracted to clean homes in his company.

Within a year, Steve had rented a small offic in town and employed an offic manager, Clarissa, to book appointments and handle the administrative side of the business. He also hired a bookkeeper, Tim, to handle the finances. Steve was ecstatic with the progress his young business had made. He celebrated by taking his wife and son on the first vacation they'd had in three years.

Of course, managing a business was more complicated and time-consuming than working for someone else. Steve not only supervised all the jobs Clarissa and Tim did in the office he was continually looking for new subs to handle the actual work in the field. It was hard to find experienced people, but it wasn't impossible. When he wasn't hiring and training, of course, he was meeting prospects in their homes, pitching his home cleaning services, or addressing this or that mistake a subcontractor had made. Then there were the daily trips to the bank, wading through customer paperwork, or speaking with vendors (which usually degenerated into *arguing* with vendors). He also found himself spending more and more time on the telephone dealing with customer complaints and nurturing relationships.

As the months went by and more and more customers came through the door, Steve had to spend even more time just trying to keep his head above water.

By the end of its second year, the company, now employing two full-time offic staff and between five and seven subcontractors to clean homes, had moved to a larger offic downtown. The demands on Steve's time had grown with the company.

He began leaving home earlier in the morning, returning home later at night. He drank more. He rarely saw his son anymore. For the most part, Steve was resigned to the problem. He saw the hard work as essential to building the "sweat equity" he had long heard about.

Money was also becoming a problem for Steve. Although the business was growing like crazy, money always seemed scarce when it was really needed.

When Steve had worked for somebody else, he had been paid twice a month. In his own business, he often had to wait - sometimes for months. He was still owed money on billings he had completed more than ninety days before.

Of course, no matter how slowly Steve got paid, he still had to pay *his* people. This became a relentless problem. Steve often felt like a juggler dancing on a tightrope. A fire burned in his stomach day and night.

To make matters worse, Steve began to feel that Peggy was insensitive to his troubles. Not that he often talked to his wife about the company. "Business is business" was Steve's mantra. "It's my responsibility to handle things at the offic and Peggy's responsibility to take care of the family."

Peggy herself was frustrated by Steve's near-constant "busy-ness" and the incredibly long hours he put in. At first, she'd wanted to work in the business, but she really didn't have the skills, and daycare costs for their son would have nearly offset what she could have earned. Later, as he'd hired subcontractors to carry out the cleaning duties, there was never really an opportunity for Peggy to play a role in the company. Sure, they had more money than before, but the costs, in terms of her and their son never seeing Steve, simply didn't seem worth it. Steve couldn't help but notice that his wife seemed resentful, and her apparent lack of understanding baffle him. Didn't she see that he had a company to take care of? That he was doing it all for his family? Apparently not.

As time went on, Steve became even more consumed and frustrated by his business. When he went off on his own, he remembered saying, "I won't have to deal with people telling me what to do." But people were still telling him what to do.

Not surprisingly, Peggy grew more frustrated by her husband's lack of communication. Their relationship grew tense and strained. The rare moments they *were* together were more often than not peppered by long silences - a far cry from the heartfelt conversations that had characterized their relationship's early days, when they'd talk into the wee hours of the morning.

Meanwhile, Tim, the bookkeeper, was also becoming a problem for Steve. Tim never seemed to have the financial information Steve needed to make decisions about payroll, customer billing, and general operating expenses, let alone how much money was available for Steve and Peggy's living expenses.

When questioned, Tim would shift his gaze to his feet and say, "Listen, Steve, I've got a lot more to do around here than you can imagine. It'll take a little more time. Just don't press me, okay?"

Overwhelmed by his own work, Steve usually backed off. The last thing Steve wanted was to upset Tim and have to do the books himself. He could also empathize with what Tim was going through, given the business's growth over the past year.

Late at night in his office Steve would sometimes recall his first years out of school. He missed the simple life he and his family had shared. Then, as quickly as the thoughts came, they would vanish. He had work to do and no time for daydreaming. "Having my own company is a great thing," he would remind himself. "I simply have to apply myself, as I did in school, and get on with the job. I have to work as hard as I always have when something needs to get done."

Steve began to live most of his life inside his head. He began to distrust his people. They never seemed to work hard enough or to care about his company as much as he did. If he wanted to get something done, he usually had to do it himself.

Then one day, the offic manager, Clarissa, quit in a huff, frustrated by the amount of work that her boss was demanding of her. Steve was left with a desk full of papers and a telephone that wouldn't stop ringing.

Clueless about the work Clarissa had done, Steve was overwhelmed by having to pick up the pieces of a job he didn't understand. His world turned upside down. He felt like a stranger in his own company.

Why had he been such a fool? Why hadn't he taken the time to learn what Clarissa did in the office Why had he waited until now?

Ever the trooper, Steve plowed into Clarissa's job with everything he could muster. What he found shocked him. Clarissa's workspace was a disaster area! Her desk drawers were a jumble of papers, coins, pens, pencils, rubber bands, envelopes, business cards, contact lenses, eye drops, and candy.

"What was she thinking?" Steve raged.

When he got home that night, even later than usual, he got into a shouting match with Peggy. He settled it by storming out of the house to get a drink. Didn't anybody understand him? Didn't anybody care what he was going through?

He returned home only when he was sure Peggy was asleep. He slept on the couch and left early in the morning, before anyone was awake. He was in no mood for questions or arguments.

When Steve got to his offic the next morning, he immediately headed for the makeshift kitchen, nervously looking for some Tylenol to get rid of his throbbing headache.

What lessons can we draw from Steve and Peggy's story? I've said it once and I'll say it again: *Every business is a family business*. Your business profoundly touches every member of your family, even if they never set foot inside your office Every business either gives to the family or takes from the family, just as individual family members do.

If the business takes more than it gives, the family is always the first to pay the price

In order for Steve to free himself from the prison he created, he would first have to admit his vulnerability. He would have to confess to himself and his family that he really didn't know enough about his own business and how to grow it.

Steve tried to do it all himself. Had he succeeded, had the company supported his family in the style he imagined, he would have burst with pride. Instead, Steve unwittingly isolated himself, thereby achieving the exact opposite of what he sought.

He destroyed his life - and his family's life along with it.

Repeat after me: *Every business is a family business.*

Are you like Steve? I believe that all small business owners share a common soul with him. You must learn that a business is *only* a business. It is not your life. But it is also true that your business can have a profoundly negative impact on your life unless you learn how to do it differently than most contractors do it - and *definitel* differently than Steve did it

Steve's home cleaning business could have served his and his family's life. But for that to happen, he would have had to learn how to master his business in a way that was completely foreign to him.

Instead, Steve's business consumed him. Because he lacked a true understanding of the essential strategic thinking that would have allowed him to create something unique, Steve and his family were doomed from day one.

This book contains the secrets that Steve should have known. If you follow in Steve's footsteps, prepare to have your life and business fall apart. But if you apply the principles we'll discuss here, you can avoid a similar fate.

Let's start with the subject of *money*. But, before we do, let's read another story, this time about a man who created a home cleaning business that works. Let's talk about Russell's journey... and yours.

CHAPTER

2

Assuming the Entrepreneur Mindset

Russell O'Connell

"The best way to predict the future is to create it."

—Peter Drucker

Anyone who has ever started a home-cleaning business likely feels *all* the challenges Steve and Peggy faced, and precious few of those businesses actually survive. Steve almost always goes back to work in another industry, and if he's lucky, he and Peggy will work out their differences. What's more, the challenges many home-cleaning businesses face— unlike many other industries—seem to be global. Steve makes the same errors in judgment in England as he would in the United States, his business falls apart in Australia as easily as it does in Europe, and he closes his company down in Singapore because of the same mistakes he'd make in Japan.

Why *is* that?

Simple—the home-cleaning industry is among the easiest to enter, with *billions* of potential clients to be served. To get started, one needs only some basic cleaning chemicals, a few inexpensive tools and supplies, and a desire to work.

"I've got a cleaning business!" our newly-minted business owner proclaims, and he or she sets off to get a few clients with a hastily created logo or business card. That's the first fatal error—they get someone to pay them for "cleaning."

I know what you might well be thinking here: "*But Russell! Isn't that the very point of owning a home-cleaning business!? To get paid?*"

Later, we'll cover why this approach is a huge mistake.

In fact, throughout this book, you're going to notice a theme that I touch on over and over again: *the vast majority of the men and women who run home-cleaning services started their business with a singular focus on quickly making some money.*

Their childhood dream wasn't to own a cleaning business; they didn't go to university to open a cleaning business; they didn't work their way up the ranks of someone else's home-cleaning company; and they didn't inherit the home-cleaning business their father, mother or grandfather created. To them, it was simply an opportunity to go out and make money on their own. Period. A hand-to-mouth approach. And, as Michael has taught us for decades, that's not the recipe for generating success in a small business. In fact, it's not really about creating a business at all.

Steve needed money, Steve cleaned a home, Steve made money. He might believe that he created a business in the process, but what he really did was to simply make a job for himself. He THOUGHT he was in business, but really he was in self–employment.

Creating a viable business—one that builds equity and enables you to scale your success and create wealth —is something quite different. My own story is a case in point

I was born in Manchester, England, and some might say it was a humble beginning. My parents were blue-collar workers, and although we got by, our family went through some relatively challenging times. So, when I was still a child, my parents took advantage of the Australian government's incentives for people to immigrate. Like many immigrants, they sought an opportunity for a better life. We moved to Australia when I was five years old—a most exciting adventure

As a boy I was inspired by my parents' hard-working ethic, and so took on all kinds of money-making activities from an early age. At age 10, I got up at 5:00 a.m. to deliver the morning paper. After school, I delivered the evening paper. On the weekends, I stacked the shelves at the local corner shop. I mowed lawns and collected beer bottles for redemption for cash. And in my teens, I graduated to working in various factories in our local area during my summer break.

I loved the independence and learned the value of money very early on in life, and being exposed to the world at large at a young age gave me a certain confidence in dealing with diffe - ent people and situations.

Thus, having become interested in business, I made the choice to study for a degree in economics at university, believing that this would be about how to start and run a company. I soon discovered that the classes were actually all too much about accounting, statistics, and charts for my taste, and my entrepreneurial spirit soon drew me out of the theoretical academic arena and back into the real world.

I had spotted an opportunity that I couldn't pass up.

Back then, before the advent of the Internet, real estate agents with properties for rent would normally advertise these in the classified section of Melbourne's newspapers or print lists of available rentals for display or collection at their office

There was a massive shortage of rentals at the time, and so, prospective tenants had to move very quickly. Which meant either racing around town to see everything that was available or hoping that they'd get lucky when calling and beat everyone else all calling in response to the same advertisement. It was a mad and frustrating scramble.

I thought there had to be a better way.

My idea was to simply do the leg work for the prospective tenants by calling hundreds of agents every day to get the latest property listings before they were advertised. These were entered on my newly acquired Apple 2 computer using a simple piece of software that I had written myself (back in those days, there was no off-the-shelf software to buy) and printed the lists on a dot-matrix printer, which took forever to spit out every report.

Yes, it was that long ago!

The result was that I could produce a list of 90% of all the available rental properties at any one time. Better still, I could refer prospect tenants to any agent or landlord who had a rental property that matched their particular desires giving them a huge advantage.

The service was free to agents, and I charged a fee to prospective tenants. It worked a treat. Soon, I had hundreds of customers a week—and next to no overheads.

The business income was almost all profit

I went on to be involved in many other types of businesses. At that age I was restless—and I had no fear of failure.

I ventured into men's fashion, with manufacturing and a small chain of retail shops in Melbourne. I then relocated to the UK, where I opened and operated nightclubs in Bristol and London. The club scene was at its peak—an absolutely fabulous time.

Next, I launched my own brand of cosmetics and built a direct-sales cosmetics company that grew to include some 3,000 agents nationwide, which I subsequently sold.

There were losses as well as wins, good times and tough ones, but one thing is for sure—I learned a lot. And I was still only in my twenties.

Then I got married and followed my wife's career move to Singapore. But, of course, I couldn't just sit there idly! Nearly as soon as we arrived, I was looking for something new.

I could quickly tell that the appetite for educational services was huge in Southeast Asia and so saw an opportunity to start running corporate speaking events. In fact, I was so sure of the potential that I went right ahead and booked a massive venue before I had even locked in any speakers!

It proved to be a winning bet.

There was a thirst for new ideas and a great curiosity about emerging trends. So, presenting the top authorities on topics such as entrepreneurship, marketing and sales, our seminars became hugely popular. They were a bit like today's TED talks, but without the online audience. This kind of event was something that you experienced in person.

As a matter of course, businesses started sending their middle and upper management to ensure that they could stay on top of the latest strategies and trends. In short order, these events were attracting upwards of 1,000 attendees from major companies in the region, with our seminars featuring top speakers like Dr. Wayne Dyer, W. Mitchell and Denis Waitley to name a few.

Over time we expanded to host seminars in Indonesia, Malaysia and Thailand. The largest of these was a tour by Tom Peters, author of the bestseller *In Search of Excellence,* who spoke in front of audiences of over 3,000 attendants. The Singapore event was held at the newly opened SunTec City. Sponsors such as American Express and Singapore Airlines lined up, and we enjoyed full media coverage in TV, radio and press through the Singapore Broadcasting Corporation, and we followed up with publication and sales of books and videos. It was quite an extravaganza.

I went on to become close friends with many of these business experts, and listening to them was a great education for me. But when I attended a talk by Michael E. Gerber, I could suddenly see everything in a new light.

Michael presented the very architecture of any successful enterprise, and after his talk, I picked up a copy of his book, *The E-Myth.*

And I couldn't put it down.

Here was the blueprint for entrepreneurialism. Reading *The E-Myth* turned me into a systems advocate, and I immediately started implementing this thinking into my own business.

By now, hosting seminars had led me to consulting for small and medium sized enterprises (SMEs) in the region, and one thing that stood out was how most CEOs complained about not finding the right people. But that was hardly ever the real issue. The true challenges lay in their *business* systems, not the people.

Leaning on the principles of *The E-Myth,* I was able to produce some extraordinary results. It was inspiring, fun and rewarding work. I got to work in a diverse range of businesses—everything from retail to manufacturing—inventing and implementing systems customised to their particular needs. It was a learning journey like no other.

The market in Southeast Asia changed in the late 90s, however, and I was also itching to implement the systems thinking into a new venture that was all mine.

It was with this mindset that I moved back to England in 1999—a new century, a new start—where I soon identified a promising opening.

The global giant Unilever had a startup that they wanted to divest themselves from: MyHome, a home-cleaning company.

They had poured huge resources into building MyHome when their initial findings revealed a market potential of over a billion dollars in the UK alone. They invested heavily in research and development, systems, infrastructure, sales and marketing. MyHome soon grew to become a leading home-cleaning business.

Luckily for me, Unilever decided, as a lot of companies do from time to time, to change their overall strategy and get back to 'core values,' and this presented an opportunity for me – which I grabbed with both hands.

In 2000, I acquired MyHome from Unilever and went to work on refining the business system. The business was still geared in the start-up phase and burning cash—but now it was *my* money that was burning —there was no time to waste – I needed to turn things around fast.

Long story short: within a few months, we had turned the business profitable. Within the next few years, we had acquired several other companies in the sector, creating a group of nine brands, with nearly a 1,000 franchise partners across nine countries.

In 2006, only six years after I had bought MyHome, the group launched a successful Initial Public Offering on the London AIM stock market, going on to achieve a market capitalization of 100 million pounds. From a money-losing small cleaning entity to a multi brand national (and international) public company in just over six years – the journey was breathtaking.

Such is the power of the principles of *The E-Myth*—if you follow them to the letter.

We'll get into how I succeeded with MyHome soon. But first I'd like to explain just why I chose this industry. Because, at the time, people were incredulous that I wanted to get into the home-cleaning business of all things.

"*Good heavens, Russell, why?*"

The reality was, I was looking for a business that was a bit different

A business that I could build so that it would work *for* me.

A business that met the standards I set and could project the values that I hold.

A business that could give me satisfaction in every area of life.

Not just a job.

Not just another paycheck.

I wanted to create something of value, and, importantly, something that appealed to the life I wanted to lead.

It started with a shopping list.

When I moved back to England from Singapore, before even looking at opportunities, I created a list of business attributes that would create the lifestyle I wanted.

This included:

- A business with a huge market that was poorly serviced—a market jampacked with frustrated customers hungry for something different
- A business in the service sector—I had had enough of retail and all the hassles and risks that come with holding stock, long expensive leases and crazy hours.
- A business that I could systemize and scale was a must.
- A business with high cash flow and excellent margins
- A business with low overheads and regular working hours —in other words, NOT in hospitality!
- A business that I could build a strong brand around which would stand out as market leader.
- A business that would always be in demand, through any economic downturn.
- A business that would enable me to train just about anyone to deliver on every last detail of our business systems.
- Nothing that would force me to travel—I was done with spending time away from the family, on red-eye flight and in lonely hotel rooms.
- Nothing that would require day-to-day selling—I wanted a recurring and steady revenue.

The actual list was a lot longer than this, but you get the idea.

As I did my research both in the UK and USA, I had observed a growing trend where more and more people were beginning to outsource tasks they didn't want to do themselves. Today, this is commonplace, of course—you outsource all kinds of services on your smartphone. But back then, this was only an emerging trend. And, on closer inspection, I had identified one particular type of service that fit the bill perfectly.

Housework.

It ticked all the items on my shopping list:

It takes precious little effort to sell home-cleaning services since demand is high (retaining customers and growing your business is another story, though), and it's a HUGE, albeit fragmented market.

- It's a business wide open to systemization and scaling.
- It's a market that transcends borders, cultures and crises.
- Despite the myriad of small companies offerin home-cleaning, the industry is truly among the most poorly serviced in the world. Owners and clients emphasize "clean", but no one can agree on what it actually means. And this causes no end of frustration for both parties. There was a huge prize waiting for the company that could ease that frustration.
- Precious few home-cleaning companies ever grow beyond the owner and a handful of employees. In fact, the number of home-cleaning companies with more than three vehicles in their fleet is virtually zero
- With almost no corporate competition, the potential for even a modestly systemized home-cleaning business is almost unlimited. Here was an opportunity for me to become THE go-to brand.
- All in all, the industry was rife with challenges—and the reward for the businesses that could solve these would be tremendous.

So, now you see my rationale for buying MyHome.

But let's get back to what I did in the beginning that set the foundations for MyHome's future success.

My team and I identified many things Michael and I will be sharing in far greater detail later, but to hit the highlights now…

First, we defined our ideal customers and shrunk the business to focus on these exclusively, which meant saying goodbye to certain customers who didn't fit the bill (and we'll share more about defining the RIGHT customers later in the book).

Next, we got very granular on the geographic areas we could serve, and began to focus our efforts there, even though it meant that some "great spots" would lie fallow. This obviously reduced travel times and overheads significantl , making the logistics of providing a superior service so much easier.

While these pieces were in motion, we also revamped our pricing structure. Up until that point, and like everyone else in the industry, MyHome had charged an hourly fee. But after discussions with our customers, we calculated that it would be better for us, and fairer for our customers, if we charged a flat rate. It would make for far greater transparency and consistency.

We insisted that customers pay us by using a credit card, which improved our cash flow and cut down on administration—and made things a lot easier and more secure for the customers.

Perhaps most importantly, we defined "*clean*", turning home-cleaning services into a *product*. Customers knew exactly what they were going to get, and the appreciation they showed for this was one of the key success factors.

Lastly, we got everybody in the company involved in making sure that we exceeded customers' expectations. We fostered a strong MyHome culture, where standardized inductions, training programs and uniforms made it easy for employees to feel part of the brand. Having an in-depth understanding of our business system, staff could really take ownership of their tasks and KPIs.

It was these kinds of strategic changes that saw MyHome grow to a group of companies with a revenue of 100 million pounds.

All from a humble home-cleaning business…

Of course, this is just a small part of the picture—we introduced a whole range of other initiatives, but the point here is that it was less about *what* we did and more about the systemic approach we took.

It was tremendously satisfying to get such a resounding confirmation of the power of systems-based thinking—and it came with all the trappings of success. I had the big house, the trips to Europe, the Aston Martin, more money than I could possibly need… the whole package.

Yet, only a couple of years later, I chose to step down as business leader and leave it all behind.

Why?

I had reached a nexus point in my life.

The events that shook the global financial system in 2008 meant that like every business the board had to take a close look at the business we had built, the changed financial landscape and the strategic options for the future direction of the business. There was a lot of work to do and a lot of options on the table.

This gave me a chance to take a closer look at the life I was leading, my role in the business and to reflect on the personal sacrifices I had made to achieve so much in such a short time. It had been quite a ride.

When it came to it, I quickly concluded that it was a good time to step back for one powerful reason.

I realized that I was not enjoying it anymore---it just wasn't me.

As a dyed-in-the-wool entrepreneur, I like creating things, and when a company gets to a certain size, it's just not the same anymore. You must report to a board, you have shareholders to appease, there are fundraising meetings and board meetings and accountancy meetings... All too often, inspiring ideas suffer death by committee.

Without really noticing this gradual shift, you suddenly find that your job description has changed drasticall .

Worst of all: you have less of what you actually want the most—time with your loved ones and for the important things that really matter.

Stephen Covey, author of 'The Seven Habits of Highly Effective People,' put it perfectly in one of his seminars, "it's incredibly easy to work harder and harder in climbing the ladder of success, only to find that it's leaning against the wrong wall!"

That's the situation I found myself in.

My daughter was about to start secondary education, I was about to turn 50, and my mother—who was still in Melbourne —was in ill health. Since it had always been our intention to return to Australia someday, we decided that now was the time to do it.

So, in 2008, we packed our bags and moved back to Australia to start a new chapter.

To break up the journey and to get some well-deserved R&R we stopped in Dubai for a few weeks to enjoy the sun. I started to plan for the future and to prepare I did what Michael has talked of so much: I sat down again with a sheet of blank paper, opened my beginner's mind and set about creating a new business from scratch:

MyHome 2.0—a different approach

One of the things I realized was just how much I love the tactile side of the business—meeting people, speaking with customers and prospects, telling the story of MyHome. Somehow, I had lost that in the UK, so I was now determined to make it a key part of the new MyHome culture.

That's not to say I dismissed or ignored the strategic side of our business, but I knew that I wanted to create a business that would give everyone involved the best quality of life—both at work and at home. A *balance.*

Sure, I could lean on systems that we had created in the UK. Times had changed by now, though. Perhaps most importantly, the Internet of Things had come through in full force, and the availability of newly emerging digital tools made for a very different future, indeed

So, as I sat there with my blank sheet of paper, it was all on the table; it was all reimagined; it was all investigated.

What eventually emerged—what is now MyHome—is the result of doing the very work Michael has said to do. Build it, break it, refine it, break it again, rebuild it bette .

Again and again and again.

...And we're still doing it to this day!

A key insight was that MyHome should be all about providing EVERYONE (not just me) —my family, our staff, our suppliers and our customers—with quality time. A better way to enjoy life. That's why our tagline became "We do clean ... you do life™".

myhome®

we do clean ... you do life

It is all about quality time--for the things that matter most.

During the course of this book, I'll return to this theme repeatedly. Because this commodity, time, is really all that we humans own. Our lives. Nothing is more precious. It will never go out of fashion. And there are customers out there who consider their time to be worth a lot of money.

Now, on that topic, let me say something here, with all due respect: most home-cleaning businesses begin because they solve the Technician's most pressing problem—the need for money. In the end, though, this business, this "job" you've created, cannot—and will not—grow until you focus on something beyond simply "money."

Yes, I understand, until you *have* money, it might be the most pressing thing, and it is certainly the focus until you do. But, as you take the actions we're sharing in this book and the money begins to truly flow into your home-cleaning business, I want to caution you that you must have a focus that extends beyond merely paying the bills—or it will all be for naught. Turn your attention to what really matters:

Your family.

Your life.

Your passions.

You've got to appreciate the immense value of these things, because until you do, simply "doing the job" will not provide you the life or the freedom you want from having your own home-cleaning company.

So, don't apply the technician's "money" mindset—adopt the entrepreneur's holistic, life-focused mindset.

As you'll see, with the right systems in place, the financial side will work itself out.

Don't believe me? Let's hear from Michael on the subject of money...

CHAPTER

3

On the Subject of Money

Michael E. Gerber

"If money is your hope for independence, you will never have it. The only real security that a man will have in this world is a reserve of knowledge, experience, and ability."

—Henry Ford

Had Steve and Peggy first considered the subject of *money* as we will here, their lives could have been radically different

Money is on the tip of every business owner's tongue, on the edge (or at the very center) of every business owner's thoughts, intruding on every part of a business owner's life.

With money consuming so much energy, why do so few home cleaning businesses handle it well? Why was Steve, like so many contractors, willing to entrust his financial affairs to a relative stranger? Why is money scarce for most home cleaning businesses? Why is there less money than expected? And yet the demand for money is *always* greater than anticipated.

What is it about money that is so elusive, so complicated, so difficul to control? Why is it that every home cleaning business owner I've ever met hates to deal with the subject of money? Why are they almost always too late in facing money problems? And why are they constantly obsessed with the desire for more of it?

Money - you can't live with it and you can't live without it. But you'd better understand it and get your people to understand it. Because until you do, money problems will eat your business for lunch.

You don't need an accountant or financial planner to do this. You simply need to prod your people to relate to money very personally. From technician to receptionist, they should all understand the financial impact of what they do every day in relation to the profit and loss of the compan .

And so you must teach your people to think like owners, not like technicians or offic managers or receptionists. You must teach them to operate like personal profit centers, with a sense of how their work fits in with the company as a whole

You must involve everyone in the business with the topic of money - how it works, where it goes, how much is left, and how much everybody gets at the end of the day. You also must teach them about the four kinds of money created by the business.

The Four Kinds of Money

In the context of owning, operating, developing, and exiting from a home cleaning business, money can be split into four distinct but highly integrated categories:

- Income
- Profi
- Flow
- Equity

Failure to distinguish how the four kinds of money play out in your business is a surefire recipe for disaste .

Important note: Do *not* talk to your accountants or bookkeepers about what follows; it will only confuse you. The information comes from the real-life experiences of thousands of small business owners, home cleaners included, most of whom were hopelessly confused about money when I met them. Once they understood and accepted the following principles, they developed a clarity about money that could only be called enlightened.

The First Kind of Money: Income

Income is the money a company pays its employees for doing their job *in* the business, *including* the owner of the home cleaning business. It's what they get paid for going to work every day.

Clearly, if the men and women you employ in your home cleaning company didn't do their job, others would have to, and *they* would be paid the money the business currently pays your team. Income, then, has nothing to do with *ownership*. Income is solely the province of *employeeship*.

That's why to the home cleaning business owner/*technician*, Income is the most important form money can take. To the home cleaning business owner/*entrepreneur*, however, it is the least important form money can take.

Most important; least important. Do you see the conflict? The conflict between the owner/technician and the owner/entrepreneur?

We'll deal with this conflict later. For now, just know that it is potentially the most paralyzing conflict in the conversation around money as you grow from a technician into an entrepreneur.

Failing to resolve this conflict will cripple you. Resolving it will set you free.

The Second Kind of Money: Profit

Profit is what's left over after your home cleaning company has done its job effectively and efficient . If there is no profit, the business is doing something wrong.

However, just because the business shows a profit does not mean it is necessarily doing all the right things in the right way. Instead, it just means that something was done right during or preceding the period in which the profit was earned

The important issue here is whether the profit was intentional or accidental. If it happened by accident (which most profit does), don't take credit for it. You'll live to regret your impertinence.

If it happened intentionally, take all the credit you want. You've earned it. Because profit created intentionally, rather than by accident, is replicable - again and again. And your business's ability to repeat its performance is the most critical ability it can have.

As you'll soon see, the value of money is a function of your business's ability to produce it in predictable amounts at an above-average return on investment.

Profit can be understood only in the context of your business purpose, as opposed to *your* purpose as the owner of a home cleaning business. Profit, then, fuels the forward motion of the business that produces it. This is accomplished in four ways:

- Profit is *investment capital* that feeds and supports growth.
- Profit is *bonus capital* that rewards people for exceptional work.
- Profit is *operating capital* that shores up money shortfalls.
- Profit is *return-on-investment* capital that rewards you, the owner / entrepreneur, for taking risks.

Without profit, a home cleaning business cannot subsist, much less grow. Profit is the fuel of progress

If a business misuses or abuses profit, however, the penalty is much like having no profit at all. Imagine the plight of a home cleaning company that has way too much return-on-investment capital and not enough investment capital, bonus capital, and operating capital. Can you see the imbalance this creates?

The Third Kind of Money: Flow

Flow is what money *does* in a home cleaning business, as opposed to what money *is*. Whether the business is large or small, money tends to move erratically through it, much like a pinball. One minute it's there; the next minute it's not.

Flow can be even more critical to a business's survival than profit, because a business can produce a profit and still be short of money. Has this ever happened to you? It's called profit on paper rather than in fact.

No matter how large your business, if the money isn't there when it's needed, you're threatened - regardless of how much profit you've made. ou *can* borrow it, of course.

But money acquired in dire circumstances is almost always the most expensive kind of money you can get.

Knowing where the money is and where it will be when you need it is a critically important task of both the owner/technician and the owner/entrepreneur.

Rules of Flow

You will learn no lesson more important than the huge impact flow can have on the health and survival of your home cleaning sole proprietorship, let alone your business or enterprise. The following two rules will help you understand why this subject is so critical.

1. The First Rule of Flow states that your income statement is static, while the flow is dynamic. Your income statement is a snapshot, while the flow is a moving picture. So, while your income statement is an excellent tool for analyzing your business *after* the fact, it's a poor tool for managing it in the heat of the moment.

Your income statement tells you (1) how much money you're spending and where, and (2) how much money you're receiving and from where.

Flow gives you the same information as the income statement, plus it tells you *when* you're spending and receiving money. In other words, flow is an income statement moving through time. And that is the key to understanding flo. It is about management in real time. How much is coming in? How much is going out? You'd like to know this daily, or even by the hour if possible. Never by the week or month.

You must be able to forecast flo. You must have a flow plan that helps you gain a clear vision of the money that's out there next month and the month after that. You must also pinpoint what your needs will be in the future.

Ultimately, however, when it comes to flo, the action is always in the moment. It's about *now*. The minute you start to meander away from the present, you'll miss the boat.

Unfortunately, few home cleaning businesses pay any attention to flow until it dries up completely and slow pay becomes no pay. They are oblivious to this kind of detail until, say, customers announce that they won't pay for this or that. That gets an owner's attention because the expenses keep on coming.

When it comes to flo, most home cleaners are flying by the proverbial seat of their pants. No matter how many people you hire to take care of your money, until you change the way you think about it, you will always be out of luck. No one can do this for you.

Managing flow takes attention to detail. But when flow is managed, your life takes on an incredible sheen. You're swimming with the current, not against it. You're in charge!

2. The Second Rule of Flow states that money seldom moves as you expect it to. But you do have the power to change that, provided you understand the two primary sources of money as it comes in and goes out of your home cleaning business.

The truth is, the more control you have over the *source* of money, the more control you have over its flo . The sources of money are both inside and outside of your business.

Money comes from *outside* your business in the form of receivables, reimbursements, investments, and loans.

Money comes from *inside* your business in the form of payables, taxes, capital investments, and payroll. Payables are the costs associated with attracting customers, delivering your services, operations, and so forth.

Few business owners see the money going *out* of their business as a source of money, but it is.

When considering how to spend money in your business, you can save - and therefore make - money in three ways:

- Do it more effectively
- Do it more efficientl
- Stop doing it altogether.

By identifying the money sources inside and outside of your business, and then applying these methods, you will be immeasurably better at controlling the flow in your business

But what are these sources? They include how you:

- Manage your services;
- Buy supplies and equipment;
- Compensate your people;
- Plan people's use of time;
- Determine the direct cost of your services;
- Increase the number of customers you see;
- Manage your work;
- Collect reimbursements and receivables.

In fact, every task performed in your business (and ones you haven't yet learned how to perform) can be done more efficiently and effectivel , dramatically reducing the cost of doing business. In the process, you will create more income, produce more profit, and balance the fl .

The Fourth Kind of Money: Equity

Sadly, few home cleaners fully appreciate the value of equity in their business. Yet equity is the second most valuable asset any owner will ever possess. (The first most valuable asset is, of course, your life. More on that later.)

Equity is the financial value placed on your home cleaning business by a prospective buyer.

Thus, your *business* is your most important product, not your services. Because your business has the power to set you free. That's right. Once you sell your business - providing you get what you want for it - you're free!

Of course, to enhance your equity, to increase your business's value, you have to build it right. You have to build a business that works. A business that can become a true business, and a business that can become a true enterprise.

A company/business/enterprise that can produce income, profit, flo , and equity better than any other home cleaning business can, in the eyes of your buyer.

To accomplish that, your business must be designed so that it can do what it does systematically and predictably, every single time.

The Story of McDonald's

Let me tell you the most unlikely story anyone has ever told you about the successful building of a home cleaning company, business, and enterprise. Let me tell you the story of Ray Kroc.

You might be thinking, "What on earth does a hamburger stand have to do with my business? I'm not in the hamburger business; I clean houses!"

Yes, you do. But by cleaning those homes, as you've figured out, as you have been taught, you've abandoned any chance to expand your reach, help more customers, or improve your services the way they must be improved if the business of home cleaning - and your life - is going to be transformed.

In Ray Kroc's story lies the answer.

Kroc called his first McDonald's restaurant "a little money machine." That's why thousands of franchisees bought it. And the reason it worked? Kroc demanded consistency, so that a hamburger in Philadelphia would be an advertisement for one in Peoria. In fact, no matter where you bought a McDonald's hamburger in the 1950s, the meat patty was guaranteed to weigh exactly 1.6 ounces, with a diameter of 35/8 inches. It was in the McDonald's Operations Manual.

Did Kroc succeed? You know he did! And so can you, once you understand his methods. Consider just one part of his story.

In 1954, Kroc made his living selling the five-spindle Multimixer milkshake machine. He heard about a hamburger stand in San Bernardino, California, that had eight of his machines in operation, meaning it could make forty shakes simultaneously. This he had to see.

Kroc flew from Chicago to Los Angeles, then drove sixty miles to San Bernardino. As he sat in his car outside Mac and

Dick McDonald's restaurant, he watched as lunch customers lined up for bags of hamburgers.

In a revealing moment, Kroc approached a strawberry blonde in a yellow convertible. As he later described it, "It was not her sex appeal but the obvious relish with which she devoured the hamburger that made my pulse begin to hammer with excitement."

Passion.

In fact, it was the French fry that truly captured his heart. Before the 1950s, it was almost impossible to buy fries of consistent quality. Kroc changed all that. "The French fry," he once wrote, "would become almost sacrosanct for me, its preparation a ritual to be followed religiously."

Passion and preparation.

The potatoes had to be just so - top-quality Idaho russets, eight ounces apiece, deep-fried to a golden brown, and salted with a shaker that, as Kroc put it, kept going "like a Salvation Army girl's tambourine."

As Kroc soon learned, potatoes too high in water content - and even top-quality Idaho russets varied greatly in water content - will come out soggy when fried. And so Kroc sent out teams of workers, armed with hydrometers, to make sure all his suppliers were producing potatoes in the optimal solids range of 20 to 23 percent.

Preparation and passion. Passion and preparation. Look those words up in the dictionary and you'll see Kroc's picture. Can you envision *your* picture there?

Do you understand what Kroc did? Do you see why he was able to sell thousands of franchises? Kroc knew the true value of equity, and, unlike Steve from our story, Kroc went to work *on* his business rather than *in* his business. He knew the hamburger wasn't his product - McDonald's was!

So, what does *your* home cleaning business need to do to become a little money machine? What is the passion that will drive you to build a business that works - a turnkey system like Ray Kroc's?

Equity and the Turnkey System

What's a turnkey system? And why is it so valuable to you? To better understand it, let's look at another example of a turnkey system that worked to perfection: the recordings of Frank Sinatra.

Sinatra's records were to him as McDonald's restaurants were to Ray Kroc. They were part of a turnkey system that allowed Sinatra to sing to millions of people without having to be there himself.

Sinatra's recordings were a dependable *turnkey* system that worked predictably, systematically, automatically, and efforlessly to produce the same results every single time - no matter where they were played, and no matter who was listening.

Regardless of where Sinatra was, his records just kept on producing income, profit, flo , and equity, over and over ... and still do! Sinatra needed only to produce the prototype recording and the system did the rest.

Kroc's McDonald's is another prototypical turnkey solution, addressing everything McDonald's needs to do in a basic, systematic way so that anyone properly trained by McDonald's can successfully reproduce the same results.

And this is where you'll realize your equity opportunity: in the way your company does business; in the way your business systematically does what you intend it to do; and in the development of your turnkey system - a system that works even in the hands of ordinary people (and other home cleaners less experienced than you) to produce extraordinary results.

Remember:

- If you want to build vast equity in your business, then go to work *on* your business, building it into a business that works every single time.
- Go to work *on* your business to build a totally integrated turnkey system that delivers exactly what you promised every single time.
- Go to work *on* your business to package it and make it stand out from the home cleaning businesses you see everywhere else.

Here is the most important idea you will ever hear about your business and what it can potentially provide for you:

The value of your equity is directly proportional to how well your business works. And how well your business works is directly proportional to the effectiveness of the systems you have put into place upon which the operation of your business depends.

Whether money takes the form of income, profit, flo , or equity, the amount of it - and how much of it stays with you - invariably boils down to this. Money, happiness, life - it all depends on how well your business works. Not on your people, not on you, but on the system.

Your business holds the secret to more money. Are you ready to learn how to find it

Earlier in this chapter, I alerted you to the inevitable conflict between the owner/technician and the owner/entrepreneur. It's a battle between the part of you working *in* the business and the part of you working *on* the business. Between the part of you working for income and the part of you working for equity.

Here's how to resolve this conflict

1. Be honest with yourself about whether you're fillin *employee* shoes or *owner* shoes.

2. As your business's key employee, determine the most effective way to do the job you're doing, *and then document that job.*

3. Once you've documented the job, create a strategy for replacing yourself with someone else (another technician, or a contractor) who will then use your documented system exactly as you do.

4. Have your new employees manage the newly delegated system. Improve the system by quantifying its effectiveness over time.

5. Repeat this process throughout your business wherever you catch yourself acting as employee rather than owner.

Learn to distinguish between ownership work and employee-ship work every step of the way.

Master these methods, understand the difference between the four kinds of money, develop an interest in how money works in your business ... and then watch it flow in with the speed and efficiency of a variable capacity compress .

Now let's take another step in our strategic thinking process. Let's look at the subject of *planning*. But first, let's see what Russell has to say about *money.*

CHAPTER

4

Making Money Your Ally

Russell O'Connell

"Risk comes from not knowing what you're doing."

—Warren Buffe

Just like your business should work *for* you, money should work *for* you, too. Not the other way around. You shouldn't work for money—at least not money alone.

Think of the classical story about the fisherman and businessman. The fisherman was relaxing at a beautiful beach, his line cast into the sparkling blue water. Suddenly a businessman, taking a break from a hectic day at the office comes up to him. "You're not going to catch many fish like that", exclaims the businessman. "You should be at work instead of just lounging on the beach!" The fisherman, smiling, replies, "And what would my reward be?" The businessman retorts, "you could make lots of money and buy yourself a whole fleet of fishing boats, catching heaps of fish". The fisherman, still smiling, says, "and what would my reward be then?" Frustrated, the businessman explains, as though to a five-year-old, "well, you'd be so rich, you could just lie on this here beach, not a care in the world, watching the beautiful scenery and enjoying life!"

"And" said the fisherman with an even bigger smile, "what am I doing right now!?"

Point being *make sure that you rule money. Don't become ruled by it.*

Money in and by itself is certainly not the "root of all evil"—it's the mindless pursuit of it that can be a bad thing. Key word: mindless. With an understanding of how money works, you can gain the control required to make it a source of freedom and enjoyment—for yourself and everyone in your business.

Unfortunately, of all the bad habits to be found in home-cleaning companies, the most universal is the relationship you, as the owner, have with money. The challenge, for most owners, is one of vocabulary. "Money" becomes a universal term for all four of the categories Michael talked about in Chapter 3.

It's most assuredly not, and until you begin to use the right terms and put "money" into its proper place within your business, you'll continuously chase it.

To truly be successful in the home-cleaning business means to recognize and learn how money fits into—and flows through—your business.

If it flows from the customer directly into your pocket, here's a hard fact: you have a job, not a business. You cannot treat your home-cleaning business as a cash machine, simply taking cash out when the mood strikes you.

As the owner, you do have a right to certain types of money, but not all of them. For example, if your business turns over $200,000, you don't personally have that. That's the *income* of your home cleaning business. As that money moves into and through your company, that *flo* isn't yours either.

Once it's done, though, the *profi*? That's yours, and so is the *equity*. Good fences make good neighbors in life, and the same is true when it comes to the money in your business.

Michael talked about the four types of money: income, profit, flo , and equity. So, let's take a deeper look at how a smart home-cleaning business can organize these different types of money into a powerful model.

Income

Income is, quite simply, the money that comes into your home-cleaning business from cleaning homes. It's also a critical growth metric for you to understand what your business can generate annually, and how much you need to charge in order to sustain and grow the company.

But—and this is a big "but"— your total income must be weighed against your total expenses. After all, the ultimate goal isn't to generate income, but to make profit and build equit .

Among other systemic changes that we made when acquiring MyHome in the UK was the decision to remove the income streams with unacceptably high expenses. That's how we made the business profitable—and a lot more manageable—in such a short time. You can think of it as prudent gardening—much like you prune a rose bush before the season, we pared back the business to create a stronger base from which to grow.

And, as mentioned earlier, we also did something else that was totally unique to the industry—we started charging a flat rate instead of hourly fees. When we implemented a new system, the Tri-colour™ cleaning process (more on this later), we could set clear expectations on what we were going to deliver.

For one thing, this made our service more attractive to customers, who appreciated knowing in advance how much they'd be paying and what level of service they were going to receive. So, it became easier to gain new customers. Secondly, it enabled us to forecast our income to the dollar—and this is incredibly important. Only by having set standards that allow you to create and predict recurring revenue can you build a scalable business system.

Speaking of scaling: growing will cost you. There will be times when you're going to have to invest in new staff, vehicles and associated overheads in order to take on any more jobs. Because you won't be using subcontractors (I'll explain why in another chapter). This is another reason to build in a steady repeatable income with solid profit margins. Sufficien profit allows you to get through these growth phases without going into the red.

As far as income is concerned, there are in reality only three ways to increase it:

Get more customers. The RIGHT customers.

Improve client retention. Meet customers' expectations.

Increase average spend per customer. Provide exceptional value—and charge for it accordingly!

Further on in this book, we'll go through how to implement strategies just like these, so that you can also achieve this kind of growth. For now, let's look at the bottom line: profit

Profit

As you begin planning your business, focus on the bottom line—your profit—first This might seem backwards, but bear with me.

When I founded MyHome in Australia, I started by identifying what ALL the costs would be. The taxes we'd pay as a company, the costs of every team member, the costs of vehicles, of training, of supplies, and of technology.

Everything.

I then calculated the budgets, individual KPIs and cash flow that would be required to build a scalable system to control these costs and ensure strong profit margins

I'd advise you to do the same. In fact, I'll go as far as to tell anyone opening their own home-cleaning business that you'll not only get these details in terms of your costs and overhead, but you'll also set up internal systems (and separate bank accounts) ahead of time to receive profits, pay expenses and handle all the business taxes, thus avoiding the temptation so many small business owners suffer from: robbing Peter to pay Paul. When money begins to flow into your business, it automatically flows to its proper place. And there is some great software out there to help you do this automatically.

Another important consideration was to budget for paying myself a salary right from the beginning. When you adopt this seemingly minor tweak and draw a paycheck, what you're actually doing is creating two independent line items, and a new philosophy.

You've now got replicable income for yourself (something many small business owners in this industry fail to achieve); you've given your home-cleaning business a separate area for profits (which, in turn, allows you to stockpile cash reserves, however modest they might be at first); and you've actively chosen to separate yourself—at least in practice—from the business.

It's a small but crucial first step toward replacing yourself as a Technician. You're moving from the limiting mindset of a self employed individual to the mindset of a business owner .

Working through this exercise, I also found it incredibly important to understand—and project—the value of each individual client. One of the good things about home-cleaning, if you do it properly, is that customers stay with you for a long time. This allows you to calculate and project revenue per customer, which we call the lifetime value, and, believe me, this puts a totally different slant on how you run your entire business

Technician-owners might go to a house, thinking, "today I'm going to make X dollars an hour cleaning this customer's home." Savvy Entrepreneur-owners, meanwhile, think, "today, my crew of technicians is servicing a customer whose lifetime value is, say, $19,500." (This lifetime value is of an example of a customer spending $250 every two weeks for three years, and when you make THIS shift in your mindset, every client becomes FAR more valuable.)

A different proposition and approach entirel .

When you assume this mindset, you'll find that your service standards become much higher! And you might be surprised by how much you can actually charge for maintaining such high standards. Charging more in turn enables you to pay your staff more and improve your standards further, leading to even greater customer acquisition and retention, expanding your business further.

You find yourself in a virtuous circle, continually growing your business and profits

We'll dig into this more elsewhere in this book, much of it in Chapter 16, but the reality is, you probably aren't charging as much as you can in your business because you refuse to see what you're *really* giving your clients: a consistent service on an ongoing basis they can trust.

If you're doing it properly, like MyHome, you're giving them care, dependability, expertise, *and you're giving them time to do the things they want to do the most.*

Flow

The beauty of understanding the hard costs of your home-cleaning business is that you'll see the flow of money through your business far easier. As Michael says, flow is constant and never-ending, and if you take the time and do the work to understand ALL the costs and how they impact you, they'll tell you exactly how and when you can expand.

Let me ask you—have you ever heard from your bookkeeper or CPA that your accounts are overdrawn, and you can't understand why?

More than likely it's because you've never stopped to look at your costs, your lack of systems, and, especially, the flow of cash through your business.

The most important thing to remember about flow is the simplest: if the cash isn't IN your business, it can't flow THROUGH your business. So, the systems you put in place to ensure continuous cash flow are incredibly important

To do that at MyHome, the solution was to simply charge the credit card that we had on file (we never accept cash). This cut out a lot of unnecessary administration and sped up our cashflow process. Today we run this via our incredibly powerful app, MyOP™, that franchise partners and team members use to verify that a home had been serviced and then automatically charges the credit card.

No invoicing, no checks, no trips to the bank, and certainly no cash to reconcile.

The transfer of funds is instant and the journey of that income through MyHome can begin immediately.

The point in all this is simple: until you make the time to understand the flow of money through your home-cleaning business, and the subsequent effects it has on profits and income, you can't really quantify how successful your own efforts will be. More importantly, you'll be cut off and removed from the last, and arguably most important point of Michael's four types of money: equity.

Equity

I believe that the only reason to go to the trouble of creating a business is to, ultimately, sell it. And to do that, the business itself naturally has to have a value: equity. But there are multiple ways to define equit , which can lead to problems later on.

Let's start by raising the standards you've probably unconsciously set for your business.

First of all, equity is not just the "stuff" your business owns. Sure, the vehicles and the equipment add to it, but the reality is, "equity" is also made up of intangibles.

It's the income, profit and cash flow we've already spoken of, as well as the expectation of what it can generate in years to come. The proof that future buyers will be looking for is in the proverbial pudding: the successful business systems that you've created.

Importantly, YOU control how equity will be defined down the road by how you treat your business today.

Let's go back to your relationship with money in our industry.

Unfortunately, most of the Technicians who own home-cleaning businesses never worry about equity—they have their blinders on, with a singular focus on making enough money for the day. The "income" simply goes right into their pockets. We've already said that's a no-no, but there's more to it than that. Between the temptation not to declare all income or to spend money frivolously under the premise of "business expenses", there is no faster way I'm aware of to lower the value of a business. Don't do it.

Seriously!

Don't. Do. It.

Boost your profits, pay the taxman, and allow those profits to show growth year after year. In time, when you're ready to exit the business, those robust profits do two things: they command a higher price for your home-cleaning business, and they ensure a higher caliber of buyer.

I often liken creation of equity to building a home. If you're building your "forever" home, you can make it incredibly personal. Have the wild colour palate, have the spiral staircase, have a tub in the master bedroom.

But if you're building that house to eventually sell, then build it to more conventional standards. Put the tub in the bathroom, build a staircase that is functional, and finish the house in colours and textures most people prefer.

Your business should be built like this—with the right kind of buyer in mind.

After all, who wants to buy a poorly managed home-cleaning company? Only another Technician, and he doesn't have any money! The person or entity you want to eventually buy your home-cleaning business wants to be shown that you've created a business that doesn't rely on you, but, rather, runs under management according to a well-defined system, producing predictable profits. And they'll pay handsomely for that

They want to see fast, easy payments.

They want a localized business that knows its core customers.

They want to see a replicable, scalable business.

I'd even go so far as to suggest you look at this potential buyer as someone who, like me, has no desire to clean homes. They're looking for income, flo , equity and profits, and—even more importantly—they're looking at how those four types of money can be grown over time.

Putting It All Together

The common thread in all this talk about money is simple: you always have, and always will have, a relationship with it. You also need to recognize that you can't change bad habits overnight, nor can you learn all there is to learn about how money works in your home-cleaning business without opening yourself up to new ideas. You've got to actively create systems and relationships with accountants and bookkeepers who can add to your education and help you understand how *this* action impacts *that* result, or how *this* investment generates *that* profit

I think of it in terms of where you wish to spend your time. You can continue to run the business like a cash machine, constantly stealing from your income and stressing about when the money will run out (and it will), or you can spend the time to master the four areas of money as Michael has taught.

Either choice takes the same amount of work!

If you choose to ignore money, you'll be left with little more than a job you've created that's taken years off your life and is worth virtually nothing. On the other hand, if you begin to master your relationship with money as an Entrepreneur and not a Technician, actively managing profits, accepting the fact that your company has to pay taxes, and really digging into the financials of your company, you will have built something amazing that has a place in the world and makes a far bigger impact than just your bank account and wealth.

CHAPTER

5

On the Subject of Planning

Michael E. Gerber

"*People in an organization operating from a creative mode... approach planning first by determining what they truly want to create, thus in essence becoming true to themselves.*"

—Robert Fritz, *The Path of Least Resistance*

Another obvious oversight revealed in Steve and Peggy's story was the absence of *true* planning.

Every person choosing to start his or her own business must have a plan. Not an idea – a real, live, tangible *plan*. You should never begin to see customers without a plan in place. But, like Steve, most people do exactly that.

A home cleaning company - and *owner* - lacking a vision is simply someone who goes to work every day. Someone who is just doing it, doing it, doing it. Busy, busy, busy. Maybe making money, maybe not. Maybe getting something out of life, maybe not. Taking chances without really taking control.

The plan tells anyone who needs to know *how we do things here*. The plan defines the objective and the process by which you will attain it. The plan encourages you to organize tasks into functions, and then helps people grasp the logic of each of those functions. This in turn permits you to bring new employees up to speed quickly.

There are numerous books, magazines, and live training seminars on the subject of home cleaning, and countless tools, widgets, and "hacks," but they focus on the technical aspects of helping you or your people *clean* better. I want to teach you something that you've never been taught before: how to be a manager. It has nothing to do with conventional business management and everything to do with thinking like an entrepreneur.

The Planning Triangle

As we discussed in the Preface, every home cleaning sole proprietorship is a business, every home cleaning business is a company, and every home cleaning company is an enterprise. The trouble with most companies owned by a home cleaning "expert" is that they are dependent on the expert. The technician/owner. That's because they're a sole proprietorship - the smallest, most limited form a company can take.

You may choose in the beginning to form a sole proprietorship, but you should understand its limitations. The company called a *sole proprietorship* depends on the owner - that is, the technician. The company called a *business* depends on other people *plus* a system by which that business does what it does. Once your sole proprietorship becomes a business, you can replicate it, turning it into an *enterprise*.

Consider the example of Vestavia Cleaning. The customers don't call in asking for Sharon Vestavia, although she has long been known in her town as the best house cleaning business around. After all, she can only handle so many calls a day and be in only one house at a time.

Yet she wants to offer these high-quality services to more people in the community. If she has reliable systems in place - systems that any qualified employee can learn to use - she has created a business and it can be replicated. Sharon can then go on to offer her services - which demand her guidance, not her presence - in a multitude of different settings. She can open dozens of home cleaning businesses, none of which need Sharon Vestavia herself, except in the role of entrepreneur.

Is your home cleaning company going to be a sole proprietorship, a business, or an enterprise? Planning is crucial to answering this all-important question. Whatever you choose to do must be communicated by your plan, which is really three interrelated plans in one. We call it the Planning Triangle, and it consists of:

- The business plan;
- The service plan;
- The completion plan.

The three plans form a triangle, with the business plan at the base, the service plan in the center, and the completion plan at the apex.

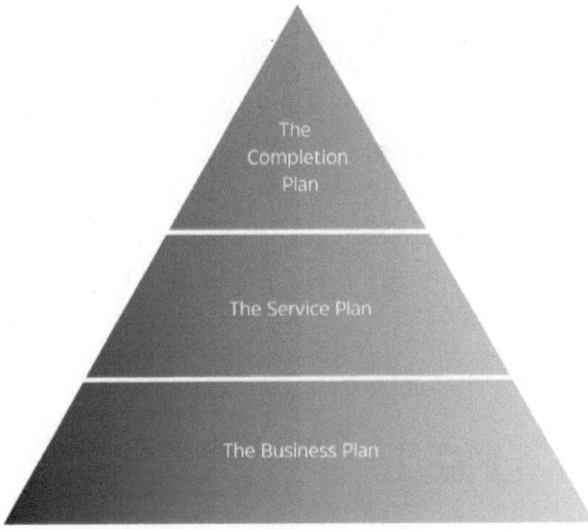

(Planning Triangle Image)

The business plan determines *who* you are (the business), the service plan determines *what* you do (the specific focus of your home cleaning business), and the completion plan determines *how* you do it (the fulfillment process)

By looking at the Planning Triangle, we see that the three critical plans are interconnected. The connection between them is established by asking the following questions:

1. Who are we?
2. What do we do?
3. How do we do it?

Who are we? is purely a strategic question.

What do we do? is both a strategic and a tactical question.

How do we do it? is both a strategic and a tactical question.

Strategic questions shape the vision and destiny of your business, of which your service is only one essential component. Tactical questions turn that vision into reality. Thus, strategic questions provide the foundation for tactical questions, just as the base provides the foundation for the middle and apex of your Planning Triangle.

First ask: What do we do and how do we do it ... *strategically?*

And then: What do we do and how do we do it ... *practically?*

Let's look at how the three plans will help you develop your service.

The Business Plan

Your business plan will determine what you choose to do in your home cleaning company and the way you choose to do it. Without a business plan, your company can do little more than survive. And even that will take more than a little luck.

Without a business plan, you're treading water in the middle of the ocean with no shore in sight. You're working against the natural flo .

I'm not talking about the traditional business plan that is taught in business schools. No, this business plan reads like a story - the most important story you will ever tell.

Your business plan must clearly describe:

- the business you are creating;
- the purpose it will serve;
- the vision it will pursue;
- the process through which you will turn that vision into a reality; and

- the way money will be used to realize your vision.

Build your business plan with *business* language, not *technical* language (i.e. the language of the home cleaning technician). Make sure the plan focuses on matters of interest to your lenders and shareholders rather than just your technicians. It should rely on demographics and psychographics to tell you who buys and why; it should also include projections for return on investment and return on equity. Use it to detail both the market and the strategy through which you intend to become a leader in that market, not as a home cleaning sole proprietorship but as a business enterprise.

The business plan, though absolutely essential, is only one of three critical plans every business owner needs to create and implement. Now let's take a look at the three legs of the business plan.

The Service Plan

The service plan includes everything a home cleaning technician needs to know, have, and do in order to deliver his or her promise to a customer on time, every time.

Every task should prompt you to ask three questions:

1. What do I need to know?
2. What do I need to have?
3. What do I need to do?

What Do I Need to *Know?*

What information do I need to satisfy my promise on time, every time, exactly as promised? In order to recognize what you need to know, you must understand the expectations and limitations of others, including your customers, administrators, technicians, and other employees. Are you clear on those expectations? Don't make the mistake of assuming you know. Instead, create a need-to-know checklist to make sure you ask all the necessary questions.

A need-to-know checklist might look like this:

- What are the expectations of my customers?
- What are the expectations of my technicians?
- What are the expectations of my staff
- What are the expectations of my vendors?

What Do I Need to *Have*?

This question raises the issue of resources - namely, money, people, and time. If you don't have enough money to finance operations, how can you fulfill those expectations without creating cash-flow problems? If you don't have enough trained people, what happens then? And if you don't have enough time to manage your business, what happens when you can't be in two places at once?

Don't assume that you can get what you need when you need it. Most often, you can't. And even if you can get what you need at the last minute, you'll pay dearly for it.

What Do I Need to *Do*?

The focus here is on actions to be started and finished. What do I need to do to fulfill the expectations of this customer on time, every time, exactly as promised? For example, what exactly are the steps to ensure the customer has a replicable and consistently clean home every time we visit?

Your customers fall into distinct categories, and those categories make up your business. The best home cleaning businesses will invariably focus on fewer and fewer categories as they discover the importance of doing one thing better than anyone else.

Answering the question "*What do I need to do?*" demands a series of action plans, including:

- the objective to be achieved;
- the standards by which you will know that the objective has been achieved;
- the benchmarks you need to read in order for the objective to be achieved;
- the function/person accountable for the completion of the benchmarks;
- the budget for the completion of each benchmark; and
- the time by which each benchmark must be completed.

Your action plans become the foundation for the Completion Plan. And the reason you need completion plans is to ensure that everything you do is not only realistic but can also be managed.

The Completion Plan

If The Business Plan gives you results and provides you with standards, The Completion Plan tells you everything you need to know about every benchmark in The Service Plan - that is, how you're going to fulfill customer expectations on time, every time, as promised. In other words, how you're going to ensure the customer's shower is always cleaned the same way, all garbage bins are emptied, cleaned, and sanitized, and all linens are changed each visit.

The Completion Plan is essentially the operations manual, providing information about the details of doing tactical work. It is a guide to tell the people responsible for doing that work exactly how to do it.

Every completion plan becomes a part of the knowledge base of your business. No completion plan goes to waste. Every completion plan becomes a kind of textbook that explains to new employees or new associates joining your team how your business operates in a way that distinguishes it from all other home cleaning businesses.

To return to an earlier example, The Completion Plan for making a Big Mac is explicitly described in the *McDonald's Operations Manual,* as is every completion plan needed to run a McDonald's business.

The Completion Plan for a home cleaning technician might include the step-by-step details of how to properly vacuum all the carpeted rooms of a home, leaving only smooth, clean carpet with no footsteps to be seen, in contrast to how a less professional company might do it. Of course, nearly everyone has used a vacuum, but they've learned to do it from their mother, or their last job, or simply because they own a vacuum. But if you are going to stand out as unique in the minds of your customers, employees, and others, you must invent your own way of doing even ordinary things. Most of that value-added perception will come from your communication skills, your listening skills, and your innovative skills in transforming an ordinary visit into a customer experience.

Perhaps you'll decide that a mandatory part of every home cleaning is to spray a specific air freshener at the end of the cleaning, and leave a small spray bottle for the client to use until your next trip out. If no other house cleaner your customer has seen has ever taken the time to do even this seemingly minor step, you'll immediately set yourself apart. You must constantly raise the questions: *How do we do it here? How* should *we do it here?*

The quality of your answers will determine how effe - tively you distinguish your business from every other home cleaning company.

Benchmarks

You can measure the movement of your business - from what it is today to what it will be in the future - using business benchmarks. These are the goals you want your business to achieve during its lifetime.

Your benchmarks should include the following:

- Financial benchmarks;
- Emotional benchmarks (the impact your business will have on everyone who comes into contact with it);
- Performance benchmarks;
- Customer benchmarks (Who are they? Why do they come to you? What will your business give them that no one else will?);
- Employee benchmarks (How do you grow people? How do you find people who want to grow? How do you cre ate a school in your business that will teach your people skills they can't learn anywhere else?).

Your business benchmarks will reflect (1) the position your business will hold in the minds and hearts of your customers, employees, and investors, and (2) how you intend to make that position a reality through the systems you develop.

Your benchmarks will describe how your management team will take shape and what systems you will need to develop so that your managers, just like McDonald's managers, will be able to produce the results for which they will be held accountable.

Benefits of the Planning Triangle

By implementing the Planning Triangle, you will discover:

- What your business will look, act, and feel like when it's fully evolved;
- When that's going to happen;
- How much money you will make.

These, then, are the primary purposes of the three critical plans: (1) to clarify precisely what needs to be done to get what the business owner wants from his or her business and life, and (2) to define the specific steps by which it will happe

First *this* must happen, then *that* must happen. One, two, three. By monitoring your progress, step by step, you can determine whether you're on the right track.

That's what planning is all about. It's about creating a standard - a yardstick - against which you will be able to measure your performance.

Failing to create such a standard is like throwing a straw into a hurricane. Who knows where that straw will land?

Have you taken the leap? Have you accepted that the word *business* and the word *sole proprietorship* are not synonymous? That a sole proprietorship relies on the individual and a business relies on other people plus a system?

Because most of these technicians are control freaks, 99 percent of today's home cleaning companies are sole proprietorships, not businesses - a fact Russell has already pointed out, and one which makes it such an incredibly great opportunity for you.

The result, as a friend of mine says, is that "these one-man businesses are spending all day stamping out fires when all around them the forest is ablaze. They're out of touch, and that sole proprietor had better take control of the business before someone else does."

Because most small business owners - especially in the home cleaning field - are never taught to think like businesspeople, the skillful technician/owner is forever at war with the businessperson. This is especially evident in the largest home cleaning companies, where bureaucrats (businesspeople) often try to control employees (the actual field technicians). They usually end up treating each other as combatants. In fact, the single greatest reason these men and women become entrepreneurs is to divorce such bureaucrats and to begin to reinvent the home cleaning business the way they "think" it should be.

That's you. Now the divorce is over and a new love affair has begun. You're a home cleaning business owner with a plan! Who wouldn't want to do business with such a person?

Now let's take the next step in our strategic odyssey. Let's take a closer look at the subject of *management*. But before we do, let's read what Russell has to say on the subject of *planning*.

CHAPTER 6

Open Your Mind

Russell O'Connell

"...most of us build prisons for ourselves and after we occupy them for a period of time, we become accustomed to their walls and accept the false premise that we are incarcerated for life."

—Og Mandino

Take a moment and read the above quote again. Surely, Og Mandino is talking about life and not business ownership, right!?

Wrong.

He's talking about *everything*, dear friend, including your home-cleaning business. Within that quote lies the truth about why MyHome was successful while so many other home-cleaning businesses failed or never provided anything more than the most modest of livelihoods for their owner.

I believe that one of the most important factors in MyHome's success to this point hasn't been my brilliance as an entrepreneur, but rather, my ignorance of what couldn't be done.

I started out not knowing what—or why—something couldn't work in our industry.

I was the ultimate beginner, and, Michael has long taught, true entrepreneurship starts with a beginner's mind and a clean sheet of paper. Thus, when I began to work on my business plan, I believe I approached it with a far different mindset than most home-cleaning business owners.

In creating MyHome, I broke things down to the very grammar of business. I refer to this as the Why, the What and the How. Sharp-eyed readers might catch this nod to Simon Sinek's phraseology, but to my linear mind, I could more easily envision the Planning Triangle.

Let's go through these concepts one by one.

Defining the Why

Most Technicians ignore the entire bottom of the Planning Triangle, if they make a plan at all. Too many times, I hear the same origination stories—the same as Steve's story—and the only "business plan" being created and executed is, "*I need to make money.*"

But making money is a *goal*, not a plan. The same could be said of any number of trivial things that go into so many "business plans", and I MUST encourage you to remove goals from this level of the Planning Triangle.

Have them in your *personal* plans, make the metrics part of your Practice Plan and your Completion Plan, *but not here.*

The "Why" is the foundation on which everything else is built. It should give every individual the company touches a clear understanding of the reason this company exists. So, it has to be straightforward and strong.

At MyHome, our Why is:

> **"Our purpose is to give people time for the things that matter most—so that the lives our customers, team members and partners are enriched and filled with more meaningful moments, experiences and memories!"**

Most Technicians don't appreciate the importance of defining and articulating the Why. To them, the Why is a waste of time, "*It's a home-cleaning business, Russell!*", they'll tell me, "*It's not rocket science! It's not a religion!*

To that, I say, "it's not *anything* if you refuse to define it, and if you refuse to proclaim and explain *why* it's necessary." What's more, if you reframe your thinking accordingly, you'll find it a lot easier to grow your business. So, stop thinking that your company exists to "clean homes" or "make money".

Refocus your thinking and aspire to create a systemized, scalable, technologically savvy business that sells time to people whose time is worth a lot.

How does that sit with you? Can you see the potential this kind of thinking opens up?

It's limitless.

It's inspiring.

It's exciting.

Defining the What

Of course, there are many ways to sell time to people whose time is worth a lot. You could be mowing lawns, detailing luxury cars or delivering ready-made meals.

Now, you'll be selling cleaning services. But there are many ways to do that, too. You could be selling end-of-lease cleaning services, carpet-cleaning services, commercial cleaning services, etc.

The What is a clear definition of *exactly what it is that you do*, to the exclusion of everything else. Once you've decided what this definition is, never ever deviate from it

Let's say, for instance, that you decide to focus, as we did, on providing residential cleaning services alone. Then don't take on the odd commercial job for a few extra dollars when the opportunity presents itself. Because anything that's not within your standards will get in conflict with your system

And always remember, *Success is in the System*™.

Notably, the What should also include a *where*. To keep your overheads low and your systems running smoothly, you should focus on the most profitable geographical areas. Don't fall for the temptation to take on new customers outside of these areas, say, accepting a customer who will pay a lot but lives half-way across the city. That too would conflict with your system, bringing unacceptable overheads in travel time, vehicle maintenance, etc.

Finally, the What includes a *who* - your ideal customer. You're going to sell time to people whose time is worth a lot. People who are happy to pay a premium for consistently great results. Don't deviate from this standard either. Don't take on customers who won't accept your rates—they're looking for cheap (read, "*subpar*") service, and that's not you. Your system depends on standards, and if you compromise on something as critical as pricing, you'll soon find yourself in a race to the bottom.

Defining the How

At the top of Michael's Planning Triangle lies the Completion Plan, which is the "How" in MyHome. This is where the cautions I mentioned in the What come into play.

The How is ***how* you do *what* you do**. It includes everything from how you run your business systems at the offic and how you pitch to prospect customer right through to the finest of details, such as how your teams of technicians wipe down a tabletop or clean a fridge. It's what makes your company better than your competition, and far more than a job you created for yourself.

Michael called it the Operations Manual for a business, and that's the truth. It includes exact definitions for every core aspect of your services—the standards and procedures for everything within your business system. This system, in turn, underpins the customer experience.

For example, just think back to the last holiday you took, and a plane flight you were on

You've got to trust the airline is going to get you and everyone else from Point A to Point B in a giant pressurized tube made up of thousands of parts and systems you likely don't understand. Your trust, therefore, will either be reinforced or curbed by what you can observe.

See the plane, gleaming on the tarmac, see the professionalism of the ground crews and the desk attendants, notice how you and the other passengers board on time, and in an orderly fashion.

Finally, you see the pilots and their sharply pressed uniforms and cordial smiles.

This entire experience is orchestrated by strictly set standards and procedures—the operations manual of the airline.

In other words, The How.

So, the How ultimately leads to the customer experience, and should thus be guided by what the customer actually appreciates most. And it's best not to make too many assumptions here. You might for instance think that it's a given that home-cleaning service customers value a clean home above all else. But that's not necessarily true.

We'll explore this further in my chapter about customers. For now, let's just look at MyHome's How, which is broadly encapsulated in the following simple statement:

Our HOW is combining the best processes, science and technology to develop incredible systems that enable our people to deliver highly professional services efficiently and consistently with amazing standards and results.

What does this mean in terms of practical measures? As an example, when I began to work on our How, I knew that I really wanted the ability for a *single digital portal* to handle everything for everyone. For our employees, for our managers, for our leaderships team—yes, even for our customers.

In time, this led to the creation of our MyOP™ app, which has taken our home-cleaning services into the 21st century, setting us apart from the rest of the industry.

Your How sets the standards you'll keep, the expectations you'll hold yourself and your future teams accountable for. The metrics you will expect employees, managers and leaders in your home-cleaning company to look for, refine and continually improve.

In summary, within the How lies everything that makes your home-cleaning company special. It's where MyHome—or any other cleaning company—can build trust by delivering great results, consistently and professionally.

How then do you create a system for ensuring that every last detail in your How works in practice and allows you to scale your business indefinitely

That's the subject for the coming two chapters.

CHAPTER

7

On the Subject of Management

Michael E. Gerber

"The most important figures that one needs for management are unknown or unknowable, but successful management must nevertheless take account of them."

—W. Edwards Deming

Every home cleaning company, including Steve Walsh's from our story, eventually faces the issues of management if they are to grow. Most face it badly.

Why do so many home cleaning businesses suffer from a kind of paralysis when it comes to dealing with management? Why are so few able to get their cleaning business to work the way they want it to and to run it on time? Why are their managers (if they have any) seemingly so inept?

There are two main problems. First, the owner usually abdicates accountability for management by hiring an offic manager. Thus, the owner is working hand in glove with someone who is supposed to do the managing. But this same business owner is unmanageable himself!

The business owner doesn't think like a manager because he doesn't think he *is* a manager. He's an owner! They started this business! "*I know how to clean houses, I don't* have *to manage - that's why I hired you!*" And so they get the offic manager to take care of stuff like scheduling appointments, keeping the calendar, collecting receivables, hiring/firing, and much more

Second, no matter who does the managing, they usually have a completely dysfunctional idea of what it means to manage. They're trying to manage people, contrary to what is needed.

We often hear that a good manager must be a "people person." Someone who loves to nourish, figure out, support, care for, teach, baby, monitor, mentor, direct, track, motivate, and, if all else fails, threaten or beat up her people.

Don't believe it. Management has far less to do with people than you've been led to believe.

In fact, despite the claims of every management book written by management gurus (who have seldom managed anything), no one - with the exception of a few bloodthirsty tyrants - has ever learned how to manage people.

And the reason is simple: *People are almost impossible to manage!*

Yes, it's true. People are unmanageable. They're inconsistent, unpredictable, unchangeable, unrepentant, irrepressible, and generally impossible.

Doesn't knowing this make you feel better? Now you understand why you've had all those problems! Do you feel the relief, the heavy stone lifted from your chest?

The time has come to fully understand what management is really all about. Rather than managing *people*, management is really all about managing a *process*, a step-by-step way of doing things, which, combined with other processes, becomes a system. For example:

- The Process for on-time scheduling
- The Process for answering the telephone
- The Process for greeting a customer
- The Process for organizing customer file

Thus, a process is the step-by-step way of doing something over time. Considered as a whole, these processes are a system:

- The On-time Scheduling System
- The Telephone Answering System
- The Customer Greeting System
- The File Organization System

Instead of managing people, then, the truly effective manager has been taught a System for managing a Process through which People get things done.

More precisely, managers and their people, *together*, manage the processes - the Systems - that comprise your business. Management is less about *who* gets things done in your business than about *how* things get done.

In fact, great managers are not fascinated with people, as our contemporary mantra suggests we must be, but instead, with how things get done through people using extraordinarily effective Systems to do it

To do that, great managers constantly ask themselves and their people key questions, such as:

- What is the result we intend to produce?
- Are we producing that result every single time?
- If we're not producing that result every single time, why not?
- If we are producing that result every single time, how could we produce even better results?
- Do we lack a system? If so, what would that system look like if we were to create it?
- If we have a system, why aren't we using it?

...And so forth.

In short, a great manager can leave the offic fully assured that it will run at least as well as it does when he or she is physically in the room.

Great managers are those who use a great management system. A system that shouts, "This is *how* we manage here." Not, "This is *who* manages here."

In a truly effective company, how you manage is always more important than who manages. Provided a system is in place, how you manage is transferable, whereas who manages isn't. *How* you manage can be taught, whereas *who* manages can't be.

When a company is dependent on *who* manages - Katie, Kim, or Kevin - that business is in serious jeopardy. Because when Katie, Kim, or Kevin leaves, that business has to start over again. What an enormous waste of time and resources!

Even worse, when a company is dependent on *who* manages, you can bet all the managers in that business are doing their own thing. What could be more unproductive than ten managers who each manage in a unique way? How in the world could you possibly manage those managers?

The answer is: You can't. Because it takes you right back to trying to manage *people* again.

And, as I hope you now know, that's impossible.

In this chapter, I often refer to managers in the plural. I know that most home cleaning businesses only have one manager—the offic manager. And so, you may be thinking that a management system isn't so important in a small cleaning company. After all, the offic manager does whatever an offic manager does (and thank God because you don't want to do it). Why go through the trouble of creating a Management System?

But if your sole proprietorship is ever going to turn into the business it could become, and if that business is ever going to turn into the enterprise of your dreams, then the questions you ask about how the offic manager manages your affairs are critical ones. Because until you come to grips with your dual role as owner and key employee, and the relationship your manager has to those two roles, your sole proprietorship/business/enterprise will never realize its potential.

Thus the need for a Management System.

The Management System

What, then, is a Management System?

The E-Myth says that a Management System is the method by which every manager innovates, quantifies, orchestrates, and then monitors the systems through which your service produces the results you expect.

According to The E-Myth, a manager's job is simple:

A manager's job is to invent the Systems through which the owner's vision is consistently and faithfully manifested at the operating level of the business.

Which brings us right back to the purpose of your business and the need for an entrepreneurial vision.

Are you beginning to see what I'm trying to share with you? That your business is *one single thing*? And that all the subjects we're discussing here - money, planning, management, and so on - are all about doing one thing well?

That one thing is the one thing your service is intended to do: distinguish your home cleaning business from all others.

It is the manager's role to make certain it all fits. And it's your role as entrepreneur to make sure your manager knows what the business is supposed to look, act, and feel like when it's finally done. As clearly as you know how, you must convey to your manager what you know to be true - your vision, your picture of the business when it's finally done. In this way, your vision is translated into your manager's marching orders every day he or she reports to work.

Unless that vision is embraced by your manager, you and your people will suffer from the tyranny of routine. And your business will suffer from it, too

Now let's move on to *people*. Because, as we know, it's people who are causing all our problems. But first let's read how Russell sorted out management in MyHome.

CHAPTER

8

Reimagining A Management System

Russell O'Connell

"Organize around business functions, not people. Build systems within each business function. Let systems run the business and people run the systems. People come and go, but the systems remain constant."

—Michael E. Gerber

I want to take a moment to acknowledge the brilliance of Michael E. Gerber, and here's why: nearly every would-be "expert" on entrepreneurship or business growth fails miserably to understand and explain "management." I'll admit, the simple—and seemingly negative—idea that people are unmanageable might feel somehow wrong in today's business and political environment, but when you embrace it as fact, it allows your home-cleaning business to grow faster, more profitably, and with far less stress.

Let me take you through MyHome and the evolution of our management system.

But first, please note that we're talking about *management* here. Not leadership. Even with a great management system, you need strong leadership. Leaders who embody the values and philosophies of your brand. You need leadership for inspiration, culture and team spirit. However, management of people, as in personally making sure that they carry out their duties, should be avoided as far as possible. Such management is a sign that your business systems aren't strong enough.

One of the reasons I have become such a student of *The E-Myth* mindset is I've always found Michael's focus on systems to be congruent with my own observations and philosophy.

As I set out to create the first management systems in MyHome many years ago, the catalysts for those systems were based on my own beliefs about what I would and would not want to "manage" as well as the long view of how our future franchisees could manage their businesses.

This single concept, the foundation of everything we have built at MyHome, began with one premise: the success we wanted must be built into the very systems we would create.

Sound familiar? It should be, Michael said it long before MyHome epitomized it!

We developed our trademark *Success in the System™* program, which is the whole foundation for how our business is run. This is enveloped in our operations manuals, which consists of six pillars, as seen in the graphic:

Delivering a Premium Service—the Tri-colour™ Cleaning System

- Managing the Money—the XERO integration
- Operational Excellence—Our proprietary MyOP™ app
- Building a Winning Team—the Hire and Inspire recruitment program
- Support and Training—the MyHome Central portal
- Winning Customers—and keeping them for life

If you take a moment to review the table of contents of this book, you'll undoubtedly note some similarities between these Six Pillars and multiple chapters within these pages.

That's no accident.

Success IS in the system, my friend. Ignore it at your own peril.

Take a moment and imagine your home-cleaning business with these same robust systems. Can you see how such systems would instantly eliminate a tremendous number of the challenges and firefightin that you face every day, from cash flo , training and customer complaints to shortage of staff and subpar standards? The list goes on and on.

Imagine a single, well-written operations manual that you and your team could all hold in your hands or pull up on a screen and see, in black and white, "*this is how we do it here.*"

How much time would that give you back, as an owner? As a leader, or a manager, or a trainer, or a salesperson, or a technician?

Naturally, it takes time to create such a work, but here's the funny thing: you could spend that time creating this system—or managing its absence. Either way, the time *will* be used. Why not use it with the long view of creating value in your business and with the knowledge that, at some point soon, the systems will be established and easily managed from there on?

Now, I've shared with you a bit of my previous experiences, but here's one that will likely shock you: I've never actually cleaned a client's home.

Not once.

I certainly could, though, because I created the systems we use, and the single most important management system we've built is the one most home-cleaning companies never even think about:

A *system* that gets a house *clean* with predictable results.

Every time.

No matter which employee is cleaning it, it is done the same way, over and over again.

That system has to be aligned with what your client expects and defines as "clean", too

Ask ten different people with ten different lifestyles what a "clean" home is and you'll receive ten (or more!) different answers. What's more important, if you ask ten home-cleaning companies to define a clean home, they'll also give you a variety of answers.

So, one of the most important aspects of the MyHome management system is the definition of *clean* and the *systemization* of delivering consistently great results, no matter who is executing it.

Definitions Create the System

The myriad of answers I got when I originally asked my ideal clients painted a clear picture: everyone wanted a clean home, but they didn't know how to define it! What was equally clear, though, was that they wanted consistent results.

That led me to the logical conclusion that if *I* could define a clean home and then explain that definition to a prospective client, they would become clients.

We'll go far deeper into this concept later, but understand, IF you own a cleaning business, as Steve found out, it's ever-so-easy to get clients, but devilishly hard to please them if your business is built on presumptions rather than standards.

Customer service is really nothing more than meeting a customer's expectations, so if those expectations aren't defined by the customer, you have an ideal opportunity to establish and define what clean is. This forms the basis for your agreement with the customer. And then?

Simply meet your own standard (and better still, *exceed it*)!

Meeting that standard, though, once you've set it for the client, is imperative.

As an example, there was a coffee shop in London I once stopped into, and when I picked up my cappuccino, I was delighted to see the initial for my name, "R", designed into the cream floating on top

Subconsciously, that set a standard I expected, and, frankly, I was somewhat disappointed when I went back a few days later and got a fantastic tasting drink, but no flourished copperplate "R" in the froth on top.

That may seem trivial, but the fact is, I'd been shown one standard as a customer only to find it not to be a standard at all. It might seem odd to mention how a well-made cappuccino could be seen as a poor customer experience, but your management systems must exist to get the right customers, set their expectations, and keep them coming back. Every time, without fail.

At MyHome, our work in this area culminated in the Tri-colour™ Cleaning System, which defines so many things within our business.

tri·colour™

What "Colour" a room is—Red Rooms (Bathrooms, Ensuites and Toilets), Green Rooms (Kitchen and Laundry) and Blue Rooms (Bedrooms, Lounge Rooms and all other Living Spaces)—denotes the specific, replicable tasks our teams will attend to in that area as well as the tactics and equipment our teams use while there.

This system of standards is incredibly precise—it describes every last detail, right down to exactly how cleaning cloths should be folded before use and after. In short, it ensures that the customer knows exactly what to expect.

Everything Flows from Tri-Colour™

Tri-colour™ also allowed us to devise an operating system to guarantee that we could deliver exactly what the customer was now expecting. It empowered us to create training and hiring systems so that an average person, with integrity and the right attitude, would know exactly what to do to meet our detailed standards in any given room or situation.

The biggest impact the Tri-colour™ Cleaning System had for us was in the consistency of the service, but perhaps not in the way you might think. Yes, that consistency meant fewer issues for managers to solve, so instead of handling issues that had occurred, it freed them up to face and address challenges that were on the horizon. Far more importantly, though, the fact that we were delivering consistent results meant that we could focus on a higher level of clientele who were willing to pay for—and truly valued—good service, and we could subtly shift the business focus to attract more such customers.

We could also train our teams in what was to be done, step by step. Thus, we could look beyond people who were skilled home cleaners and concentrate on hiring people with more important attributes—honesty, integrity, motivation, and so on—and turn THAT into a feature of our business.

Systems Must Always Evolve

As Michael said in the previous chapter, a management system is how you, and then your managers, innovate, quantify, orchestrate, and then monitor every system in your cleaning business.

Therefore, when your business evolves, so must your systems. And today, most of these systems can be digitised and automated.

At MyHome, scheduling, billing, hiring, payroll, training, hourly labor tracking, even our various cash flow and income statements, have all been brought into one place—our MyOP™ app.

Sure, your business might not yet have this level of technology in place, but rest assured, you WILL need to make changes, and this implies that, yes, you'll need a system for keeping your standard operating procedures up to date.

Getting Back Your Sundays

As you begin to create and refine your management system, there's one critical thing you must ensure: *it cannot be harder to follow correctly than it is to ignore.* For most home-cleaning business owners, if they have a system, it's poorly designed at best and, more likely, simply broken or too hard to use.

Their days off—if they have them at all—are spent sending invoices, figuring out schedules, ordering supplies and trying to figure out where all their money has gone

Simply realizing that challenge—and creating a solution—represented a huge windfall for MyHome in terms of the time and effort our managers (and then franchisees) had to spend to run their operations. Yes, I was able to create an incredible app to take care of much of this, but in your business?

You've still got options.

Cloud based SAAS (software as a service)and other affordable digital technology is readily available to automate everything from scheduling and marketing to social media campaigns and invoicing.

You owe it to yourself and your business to learn what options are currently available, use them, and determine the best ways to incorporate them into your business.

If there's a better way to do something, you should be the first to identify the opportunity and implement it. This is a core difference between echnicians and Entrepreneurs.

Technicians don't realize that they're part of a constantly evolving business ecosystem where only the fi - test survive—they are reactive, always just trying to stay afloat by applying whatever ad-hoc measure they think the current situation requires. Entrepreneurs, by contrast, understand how the ecosystem works and plan ahead—always, always looking for new ways to improve.

That's how you, the Entrepreneur, become and stay a dominating force.

CHAPTER

9

On the Subject of Employees

Michael E. Gerber

"When you innovate, you've got to be prepared for people telling you that you are nuts."

—Larry Ellison, founder of Oracle Corporation

Every business owner in the home cleaning industry I've ever met has complained about people.

About employees: "They come in late, they go home early, they have the consistency of an antique boiler!"

About managers: "They're living in a nonparallel universe!"

About customers: "They want to pay like it was 1979!"

People, people, people. Every business owner's nemesis. And at the heart of it all are the people who work for you.

"By the time I tell them how to do it, I could have done it twenty times myself!"

"How come nobody listens to what I say?"

"Why is it nobody ever does what I ask them to do?"

Does this sound like you?

So, what's the problem with people? To answer that, think back to the last time you walked into the offic of a business that handles home cleaning. What did you see in the employee's faces?

Most people working in the home cleaning industry are harried. You can see it in their expressions. They're negative. They're tired. They're humorless. And with good reason! After all, they're surrounded by people who have dirty homes, lackadaisical cleaning habits, or - worst-case scenario - people who don't lift a finger to clean their own homes, expecting the cleaning crew to do it all! Customers are looking for the most value for the least amount of money. And many are either angry or frightened. They don't know what "clean" is, or how to do it, but they all want it.

Is it any wonder employees at most home cleaning businesses are disgruntled? They're surrounded by unhappy people all day. They're answering the same questions 24/7. And most of the time, the owner has no time for them. He or she is too busy leading a dysfunctional life.

Working with people brings great joy - and monumental frustration. And so it is with owners and their employees. But why? And what can we do about it?

Let's look at the typical owner of a home cleaning business - who this person is and isn't.

Most of them are unprepared to use other people to get results. Not because they can't find people, but because they are fixated on getting the results themselves. In other words, most of the people who own a home cleaning company are not the businesspeople they need to be, but *technicians suffering from an entrepreneurial seizure.*

Am I talking about you? What were you doing before you became an entrepreneur?

Were you downsized from your last company and decided that home cleaning would be an "easy" business to break into? Maybe you worked in housekeeping in the hotel industry until the downturn in the economy left you looking for more income? Or just doing odd jobs here and there?

Didn't you imagine owning your own business as the way out?

Didn't you think that because you knew how to do the technical work - because you knew so much about cleaning your own home - that you were automatically prepared to create a business that does that type of work?

Didn't you figure that by creating your own business you could dump the boss once and for all? How else to get rid of that impossible person, the one driving you crazy, the one who never let you do your own thing, the one who was the main reason you decided to take the leap into a business of your own in the first place

Didn't you start your own business so that you could become your own boss?

And didn't you imagine that once you became your own boss, you would be free to do whatever you wanted to do - and to take home *all* the money?

Honestly, isn't that what you imagined? So, you went into business for yourself and immediately dove into the work.

Doing it, doing it, doing it.

Busy, busy, busy.

Until one day you realized (or maybe not) that you were doing *all* of the work. You were doing everything you knew how to do, plus a lot more you knew nothing about. Building sweat equity, you thought.

In reality, a housekeeper suffering from an entrepreneurial seizure.

You were just hoping to make a buck in your own business. And sometimes you did earn a wage. But other times you didn't. You were the one signing the checks, all right, but they went to other people.

Does this sound familiar? Is it driving you crazy?

Well, relax, because we're going to show you the right way to do it this time.

Read carefully. Be mindful of the moment. You are about to learn the secret you've been waiting for all your working life.

The People Law

It's critical to know this about the working life of home cleaners who own their own business: *Without people, you don't own a company, you own a job*. And it can be the worst job in the world because you're working for a lunatic! (Nothing personal—but we've got to face facts.)

Let me state what every small business owner knows: Without employees, you're going to have to do it all yourself. Without human help, you're doomed to try to do too much. This isn't a breakthrough idea, but it's amazing how many technicians ignore the truth. They end up knocking themselves out, ten to twelve hours a day. They try to do more, but less actually gets done.

The load can double you over and leave you panting. In addition to the work you're used to doing, you may also have to do the books. And the organizing. And the filing. You'll have to do the planning and the scheduling. When you own your own business, the daily minutiae are never-ceasing - as I'm sure you've found out. Like painting the Golden Gate Bridge, it's endless. Which puts it beyond the realm of human possibility. Until you discover how to get it done by somebody else, it will continue on and on until you're a burned-out husk.

But with others helping you, things will start to drastically improve. If, that is, you truly understand how to engage people in the work you need them to do. When you learn how to do that, when you learn how to replace yourself with other people - employees trained in your system - then your business can really begin to grow. Only then will you begin to experience true freedom yourself.

What typically happens is that a house cleaner running his or her own business, knowing they need help answering the phone, filing, and so on, will go out and find people who can do these things. Once they delegate these duties, however, they rarely spend any time with the hoi polloi. Deep down, they feel it's not important *how* these things get done; it's only important that they get done.

They fail to grasp the requirement for a system that makes employees their greatest asset rather than their greatest liability. A system so reliable that if Chris dropped dead tomorrow, Leslie could do exactly what Chris did. That's where the People Law comes in.

The People Law says that each time you add a new person to your business using an intelligent (turnkey) system that works, you expand your reach. And you can expand your reach almost infinitely!

People allow you to be everywhere you want to be simultaneously, without actually having to be there in the flesh

Employees are to a home cleaning business what a record was to Frank Sinatra. A Sinatra record could be (and still is) played in a million places at the same time, regardless of where Frank was. And every record sale produced royalties for Sinatra (or his estate).

With the help of other people, Sinatra created a quality recording that faithfully replicated his unique talents, then made sure it was marketed and distributed, and the revenue managed.

Your employees can do the same thing for you. All *you* need to do is to create a "recording" - a system - of your unique talents, your special system of cleaning your client's homes, and then replicate it, market it, distribute it, and manage the revenue.

Isn't that what successful business people do? Make a "recording" of their most effective ways of doing business? In this way, they provide a turnkey solution to their customers' problems. A system solution that really works.

Doesn't your business offer the same potential for you that records did for Sinatra (and now for his heirs)? The ability to produce income without having to go to work every day?

Isn't that what your employees could be for you? The means by which your system for successfully cleaning a home could be faithfully replicated?

But first you've got to have a system. You have to create a unique way of doing business that you can teach to your employees, that you can manage faithfully, and that you can replicate consistently, just like McDonald's.

Because without such a system, without such a "recording," without a unique way of doing business that really works, all you're left with is people doing their own thing. And that is almost always a recipe for chaos. Rather than guaranteeing consistency, it encourages mistake after mistake after mistake.

And isn't that how the problem started in the first place? Employees doing whatever *they* perceived they needed to do, regardless of what you wanted? Employees left to their own devices, with no regard for the costs of their behavior? The costs to you?

In other words, employees without a system.

Can you imagine what would have happened to Frank Sinatra if he had followed that example? If every one of his recordings had been done differently? Imagine a million diffe-ent versions of "My Way." It's unthinkable.

Would you buy a record like that? What if Frank was having a bad day? What if he had a sore throat?

Please hear this: The People Law is unforgiving. Without a systematic way of doing business, people are more often a liability than an asset. Unless you prepare, you'll find out too late which ones are which.

The People Law says that without a specific system for doing business; without a specific system for recruiting, hiring, and training your employees to use that system; and without a specific system for managing and improving your systems, your business will always be a crapshoot.

Do you want to roll the dice with your business at stake? Unfortunately, that is what most home cleaning businesses are doing.

The People Law also says that you can't effectively delegate your responsibilities unless you have something specific to delegate. And that something specific is a way of doing business that works!

Frank Sinatra is gone, but his voice lives on. And someone is still counting his royalties. That's because Sinatra had a system that worked.

Now we will move on to the subject of *subcontractors*. But before we do, let's see what Russell has to say about *employees*.

CHAPTER

10

Investing in the Right Employees

Russell O'Connell

"Wax on, wax off. Breathe in through nose, out the mouth.   ax on, wax off. Don't forget to breathe, very important.

—Mr. Miyagi, The Karate Kid

Most home-cleaning companies look for people who think they already know how to clean a home. They look for "experienced" people, card-carrying experts, rigorously trained professional cleaners. But—think about it—that's really a bit like McDonald's setting out to find people who are expert in making perfect hamburgers.

The simple truth of the matter is, the majority of your team *does not need* to be experts. In fact, they need to be the opposite. You should hire people who are ready—and have the personal integrity and honour—to learn and work to YOUR system.

Let me ask you *again*: how important are those systems to you and your home-cleaning company?

Remember, Michael's a "systems guy."

I'm a "systems guy."

If you choose to focus on people as a critical asset to your home-cleaning business (which they most certainly are), then you must create solutions and paths for your recruiting, hiring and training processes. One needs only read our Mission Statement to see how important this is:

"*MyHome combines the best processes, the best science, and the latest technology to develop world-leading systems for consistently high standards and results.*

These systems enable our franchisee partners and teams to deliver premium home-cleaning services to discerning customers—people who value a beautifully clean home and the time to enjoy it!"

Create the systems and teach your people how to use them, and you'll ensure that your customers' expectations are met.

A Passionate Novice

Now, in Chapter 8—and in fact at several other points in this book—you've seen the challenges that the wrong mindset can create for you as the owner of a home-cleaning business. A Technician opens a cleaning company, yet cannot define "clean" for his or her customers, much less themselves, and then, as growth demands, they hire cleaning staff—and they have the knee-jerk reaction to look for people who already have *their own* approach to cleaning.

On the one hand, it's a *systems* problem—notably, the lack of any in the business—but on the other, it's a huge *people* problem. Just look at the way most home-cleaning companies hire!

The individual whom the technician hires has been cleaning homes for years—it says so on their CVs—so "they clearly must know how to do it," and IF (and that's a *big* IF) the technician trains their new team member at all, the training is all "shadowing" or "on the job" nonsense for a few homes, then the new hire is cut loose to fend for themselves.

Is it any wonder those hires usually don't pan out?

Two things can happen here: either the customers are happy with the way a particular new cleaner does the job and will insist on having this very person service them every time (cleaning to *their own standards)*; or, they're not happy, and they'll insist on having someone else—usually, that means you, the Technician/owner—step in and do the cleaning.

Thus, our Management System from Chapter 8 must flow seamlessly into how we hire, train, and retain our people

When I speak with people about MyHome—be they potential franchise partners, employees, stakeholders or prospective clients—one of the things they're struck by is the fact we actively look for inexperienced candidates.

It's true, and for MyHome, it works splendidly.

Why? Simple. We know from what the customers have told us, that they value consistency. So, we've put the systems in place to turn a total novice into someone who can clean homes to our very exact standards every single time.

A New Concept: The Ideal Employee

Now, for years, Michael has written about the roles people play, and how people are universally hard to manage, and at MyHome, we took his teachings a step further. Not only did we acknowledge the importance of robust training systems focused on teaching average people to do an extraordinary job, we also looked at where those people could be found.

Companies worldwide—even small cleaning companies—naturally invest a lot of time, effort and money in their customers. But they often forget to apply the same focus to their staff. At MyHome, we believe that you should treat your employees just like you treat your customers.

Remember, your customers will never be happier than your employees.

And, just as you have an ideal customer, there's also an ideal employee.

For us, that's a young person with a decent degree of fi-ness, who isn't necessarily looking for a career right now—but they are looking for a good job that meets their immediate needs. A morally upright, self-motivated person who isn't looking to be defined by their job. Qualities they must have include integrity, punctuality, good communication skills, honesty, reliability and being able to follow a system.

We don't hire CVs—we hire people who have the same values as we do.

The reason is simple: our cleaners are the ones who interface with our customers far more often than our managers, our franchise partners or our support teams. They are truly the ambassadors of our brand.

At MyHome, we imbue our team members—from Day One—with a sense of belonging. We don't need highly skilled people, but we do need people who feel like they're an integral part of our business. People who take ownership of everything that they do.

We want people who are willing to row the boat with us, not go it alone and run their own race. Our whole recruitment, onboarding and management process revolves around this.

We call that system "Hire and Inspire™."

This is worlds apart from the traditional ways of technician-run cleaning companies.

Technicians hire people who've got lots of cleaning experience on their CV—and thus have their *own* ways of cleaning—and send them on their merry way, *hoping* that they will somehow produce consistent results. MyHome hires people based on values, trains them in our systems, and consistently checks that they deliver to our detailed standards.

Technicians get staff or subcontractors in on a casual basis, so that there's little chance for their cleaners to learn their standards—if they have any set standards at all, that is. MyHome hire proper employees and give them the whole package—steady income, holiday pay, pension contributions, and sick benefits—so that our staff become *part of* MyHome, embracing our values and standards.

Technicians let staff use their own clothes, vehicles, cleaning equipment and supplies (unless they use whatever they find at the customers' homes). MyHome provide clean, branded uniforms and vehicles as well as all cleaning equipment and supplies, with all cloths cleaned and folded on a daily basis.

The outcomes in terms of both branding and service delivery are, unsurprisingly, vastly different

But it's also a question of fairness. If you want your staff to provide a great service, you have to give them great service, too. They should feel that you truly care for them, and they should have a means of *knowing* that they're doing a great job. And they can only know that if you have detailed standards for what they should achieve.

Again: *Success is in the System™*.

Now, how do we FIND these people?

A good rule of thumb here: the harder you make it for people to join your business, the easier it will be to train them in your systems. (I was about to write, "the easier they'll be to manage"—see there how entrenched this thinking is even with a systems person such as myself? We are conditioned to believe that you have to hire AND manage people, when much of the point of your system is that it should free you from having to manage people…) So, to join MyHome, you have to go through a rigorous recruitment process, which includes three separate interviews, video presentations, and an induction program before you're even offered the job

This whole process is designed to draw out the values we discussed earlier. We share the MyHome story, we go over the Tri-colour™ Cleaning System, and we talk about the values that we and our customers hold dear. And we look at how they react to what we say. Does our story resonate with them? Do they appear actively interested? Are they ready to learn our systems? You can tell a lot by their body language, and by what questions and comments they make. Watch and listen carefully, and you'll soon know whether you're looking at a winning candidate.

Of course, this isn't only about vetting candidates—it's also about selling them on the job. And MyHome offers a lot that's attractive to energetic , driven people. Good benefits, a reliable schedule, daytime hours, no work on weekends and great support by digital tools (something that's second nature to new generations).

We also offer a degree of autonomy, so that our staff can take ownership of what they do. Having said that, we still see our team members every morning, without fail, for a face-to-face briefing before they head out. We're also in touch with them throughout the day, and we have the checks and balances in place to ensure that they deliver to our standards. Because it's important that everyone feels seen, thinks of themselves as part of the team, and gets feedback on what they accomplish.

Also, remember your team will *expect* what you *inspect*. And vice versa.

All of this naturally takes effort and time. As for the interview and induction process, we probably go through ten people for every hire—but it pays off in spades. We end up with employees who have the integrity and motivation to learn and deliver to our standards. Young, enthusiastic people with big plans for the future—oftentimes , we are a temporary stopgap on their journey to becoming doctors, lawyers, or scientists. And they have the dedication and professionalism it takes to achieve such high goals. They have great presentation skills, and they take pride in succeeding in *anything* that they take on.

But will you be able to keep a future doctor employed in your home-cleaning business long-term? No, you won't. And it doesn't matter. MyHome have the planning systems in place to never hire out of desperation, and training programs that run like clockwork when we do take on new staff. They hit the ground running from day one.

So, it's perfectly fine that most of our staff stay with us for less than a year, as we plan for that. After that, they're on to bigger things, and we wish them all the best!

An Endless Source of Applicants

Speaking of recruitment, I stumbled on a bit of a treasure trove for finding team members, and I'm hesitant to share here, lest you think this is the single key to our success.

It's so simple as to be almost embarrassing.

Referrals.

Our *team* began to generate new applicants.

Certainly, we still had marketing focused on hiring the right people, but the very people we hired became proponents of the work they were doing.

We trained them, we fulfilled their current needs, and we treated them well—and they told others about the great experience they had with MyHome, inspiring their friends to join our team.

Let me give you an example:

Say you've got an incredible team member named Mary. She's always on time, you've never had an issue with any of her customers, and she's got long-term goals outside of cleaning homes.

Now, how do you get more "Marys"?

Guess what? Mary has friends, and a great many of them share similar attributes.

Over the years, we've hired many such friends, and it has worked so well, we've created a system for our staff to share—on social media—not only their experience with MyHome, but also a QR code for job applications. And when we hire someone, that QR code allows us to send the referring team member a little reward for their help.

Hundreds of applicants have joined our team this way. Attracted by the many benefits outlined above, MyHome stands in stark contrast to other options available to them, and word spreads far and wide. In fact, we normally have way more applicants than we have openings, and we hire almost exclusively through referrals now. Our reputation as a quality employer has built to a point where we even receive applications from working holiday makers from overseas before they even arrive in Australia!

In closing this chapter, keep that image of "Mary" in your mind's eye: energetic, driven, with high aspirations for a future career, well-presented and eager to learn and succeed in anything she does. This person plays in a different league than the vast majority of the people we're going to talk about next.

Subcontractors.

CHAPTER

11

On the Subject of Subcontractors

Michael E. Gerber

"Meaningful relationships and meaningful work are mutually reinforcing, especially when supported by radical truth and radical transparency."

—Ray Dalio

If you're a sole practitioner - that is, you're selling only yourself - then your home cleaning company, called a sole proprietorship, will never make the leap to a home cleaning business called a company. The progression from sole proprietorship to business to enterprise demands that you hire other technicians to do what you do (or don't do). In some cases, these people might be subcontractors.

Subcontractors are different from regular employees in every country. They operate under different laws and regulations as owners of their own solely-owned company. No matter what name they operate under, they too, must operate within your System. To the degree they don't, you're in trouble.

Contractors know that subs can be a huge problem, but many small business owners refuse to recognize this special business problem, ignore it and your sole proprietorship will never become a business, and your business will certainly never become an enterprise.

Long ago, God said, "Let there be contractors. And so they never forget who they are in my creation, let them be damned forever to hire people exactly like themselves." Enter the subcontractors.

Solving the Subcontractor Problem

Let's say you're about to partner with a subcontractor. Someone who has specific skills applicable in your home cleaning business. It all starts with choosing the right personnel. After all, these are subcontractors to whom you are delegating your responsibility and for whose behavior you are completely liable. Remember Frank Sinatra? Do you really want to leave that choice to chance? Are you that much of a gambler? I hope not.

If you've never worked with your subcontractor, how do you really know he or she is skilled? For that matter, what does "skilled" mean?

For you to make an intelligent decision about this subcontractor, you must have a working definition of the word *skilled*. Your challenge is to know *exactly* what your expectations are, then to make sure your other subcontractors operate with precisely the same expectations. Failure here almost assures a breakdown in your relationship.

I want you to write the following on a piece of paper: "By *skilled*, I mean ..." Once you create your personal definition, it will become a standard for you and your business, for your customers, and for your subcontractors.

A standard, according to *Webster's Eleventh*, is something "set up and established by authority as a rule for the measure of quantity, weight, extent, value, or quality."

Thus, your goal is to establish a measure of quality control, a standard of skill, which you will apply to all your subcontractors. More importantly, you are also setting a standard for the performance of your company.

By creating standards for your selection of other subcontractors - standards of skill, performance, integrity, financial stability, and experience - you have begun the powerful process of building a company that can operate exactly as you expect it to.

By carefully thinking about exactly what to expect, you have already begun to improve your business.

In this enlightened state, you will see the selection of your subs as an opportunity to define what you (1) intend to provide for your customers, (2) expect from your employees, and (3) demand for your life.

Powerful stuff, isn't it? Are you up to it? Are you ready to feel your rising power?

Don't rest on your laurels just yet. Defining those standards is only the first step you need to take. The second step is to create a *Subcontractor Development System*.

A Subcontractor Development System is an action plan designed to tell you what you are looking for in a subcontractor. It includes the exact benchmarks, accountabilities, timing of fulfillment, and budget you will assign to the process of looking for subcontractors, identifying them, recruiting them, interviewing them, training them, managing their work, auditing their performance, compensating them, reviewing them regularly, and terminating or rewarding them for their performance.

All of these things must be documented - actually *written down* - if they're going to make any difference to you, your subcontractors, your managers, or your bank account!

Now, lest you think this only applies to the people in your home cleaning business that are cleaning homes, it doesn't. In fact, Russell has a very unique take on subcontractors, given his business' location, but a part-time bookkeeper is, in fact, a subcontractor of your home cleaning business.

... or someone who specializes in steam cleaning carpets for your customers might be, too.

...or maybe a duct cleaning company, or a business specializing in tile floor restoration, or a pressure washing business.

And then you've got to persist with that system, come hell or high water. Just as Ray Kroc did at McDonald's. Just as Walt Disney did at Disneyland. Just as Sam Walton did at Walmart.

This leads us to our next topic of discussion: the subject of *estimating*. But first, as I mentioned earlier, let's look at the approach Russell took with MyHome to solve the challenges presented by *subcontractors*.

CHAPTER

12

Don't Let Others Edit Your Recipe for Success

Russell O'Connell

"*Too many cooks spoil the broth.*"

—Some Smart Person, way back in the 16th century

If you want to build a brand, you shouldn't use subcontractors to carry out the services in your home-cleaning business. There's a simple reason for this: when people have *their own ideas* about how to do things, when they *get creative* on the job, you can never ensure the consistency that underpins your brand.

Remember what Michael said about McDonald's earlier? It's all about systems and standards to ensure a consistent customer experience. A Big Mac is a Big Mac is a Big Mac. No matter whether you're in Singapore or Paris.

McDonald's would never relinquish control of their recipes to any "seasoned burger chefs." Nor would they allow franchisees to set up their kitchens in their own way or let staff at differentrestaurants wear differentuniforms. Everything is standardized. Everything is systemized. Everything is controlled.

This is McDonald's recipe for success, and they feed their "little money machine" with young, inexperienced staff whom they train in their systems.

Your home-cleaning business should work like this, too. To continue on the restaurant analogy, you can boil everything down to this golden rule:

You *create*—others *execute*.

You create the standards. *You* create the system. *You* create the controls that ensure compliance. Others simply execute accordingly. They should never be in doubt about how to deliver your services. They should never get creative. They just do *exactly* what they're supposed to do.

Standards, standards, standards.

Now, most subcontractors are going to be "seasoned cleaners," but that also means that they already have *their own* standards. They're used to cleaning in a particular way, which will invariably differ from your standards—and this is hardwired into their very bodies. So, even if you attempt to train a subcontractor to adhere to *your* standards, you'll find it a lot harder to do so than with a novice person.

Also, there's an elephant in the room: if you're considering using a subcontractor, you're probably in a situation where you're looking for someone urgently. Your business has suddenly taken on one more customer than you can handle, or an existing staff member is off sick, and you need a customer's home cleaned pronto. There is no time for any interviewing, induction or training process (which in itself is a sign of a broken system).

So, you hire the subcontractor and *hope* that they'll do a good job.

And what if they do!? What if the customer loves the way this subcontractor cleaned their home and insists on only using them going forward? That's also a problem.

Because if you're in this situation at all, you're probably a Technician operating a small business. There's little for the subcontractor to lose by poaching your customer—and even if they don't, how will you be able to guarantee the customer that they'll be serviced by the same subcontractor every time?

This brings us to another important point: relationships.

Remember, subcontractors are *running their own business*, not yours. They are not aligned with your business nor your values; it is a purely monetary arrangement. You've seen this before: a company gets a job, then simply subs it out to someone else via a text, an email, or a phone call.

There's no *relationship* at all.

This issue is evident from the very definition of the word "subcontractor," which means to let someone else do the work that you are contracted to do—i.e., in the home-cleaning business to let someone else replace the person whom the customer entrusted with the keys to their home.

Without telling the customer about it…

Does that leave you with a sinking feeling in your stomach? It's there for a reason.

MyHome is—and your home cleaning business should be—*built* upon relationships: relationships with clients, with teams, with everyone involved in any part of the business. Without a relationship, there's no trust, because there isn't really anyone to be trusted.

Bottom line: aside from the risk of losing customers and the complete absence of a relationship, whether they underperform or overperform, subcontractors are bound to deliver to a different standard than yours. And when that happens, your system—your recipe for success—breaks. End of story.

Do not use subcontractors.

But, but, but… isn't there ANY place for subcontractors?

At the risk of sounding like a broken record: no.

There are naturally roles within your business where you want staff to make their own choices based on their own expert skills. Roles like accountant, marketing creative and lawyer. The nature of their work is such that they cannot simply follow your system. They have to *think* and *make choices* for your business. And whilst your business is still relatively small, there's hardly any need to employ an accountant, for example.

So, sure, go ahead and outsource those roles.

What you're doing here, though, is not hiring subcontractors. You're hiring consultants and freelancers. There's no contract that you *subcontract* out to someone else. There's only one contract—the one between you and the consultant or freelancer.

Which means that there's also a direct relationship to build and nurture. This is important, because you want to make sure that your consultants and freelancers share your work ethics and that they understand your systems and team culture.

You're looking for consultants who mirror your own dedication, your reliance on systems—people who understand what your business is really about. In some ways, you'll need to vet them just as you'd vet a prospective team member, but in the light of the role they'll be playing. Do they use the best practices of their industry or craft? Do they use industry-level software or something they've cobbled together over the years?

At MyHome, we have a documented system for how to assess and create solid relationships with consultants and freelancers.

Speaking of relationships—it's old news that you can get a bookkeeper overseas, or a social media manager on the other side of the world, and many times, those people *would* be excellent at what they do. But it will be a lot harder to build rapport and ensure that they really understand your business if you cannot meet in person. Also, your home-cleaning company is part of the local community. Why not support other local business? I have found great consultants and freelancers in Melbourne, and I enjoy sitting down with them, face to face, to discuss next month's plans, the budget for next year or whatever else is on the agenda.

Now, to segue into the following two chapters, think about what a relationship is. It's knowing someone—knowing what to expect from them. There's a feeling of trust, of certainty. And what we'll be covering next is something quite different. Because we'll essentially be talking about the question of *uncertainty*.

Estimations.

CHAPTER

13

On the Subject of Estimating

Michael E. Gerber

"*You can't manage what you can't measure.*"

—Peter Drucker

One of the greatest weaknesses of the home cleaning industry as a whole is accurately estimating how long jobs will take and then scheduling their customers accordingly. *Webster's Collegiate Dictionary* defines estimate as "a rough or approximate calculation." Anyone who has actually cleaned a home knows that those estimates can be rough indeed.

Do you want to see someone who gives you a rough approximation? What if your doctor gave you a rough approximation of your medical condition?

The fact is, we can predict many things we don't typically predict. For example, there are ways to calculate common problems. Look at the steps of the process. Most of the things you do are standard, so develop a step-by-step system and stick to it.

In my book *The E-Myth Manager*, I raised eyebrows by suggesting that doctors eliminate the waiting room. Why? You don't need it if you're always on time. The same goes for a home cleaning company. If your system doesn't require the home-owner to be there, then your customers don't have to wait.

What if a house cleaner made this promise: "Our teams are fully vetted and insured, thus, you can trust us to clean your home without you there. We can offer a replicable cleaning, every time, without worry, or we pay for it."

"Impossible!" the Technicians will cry. "We can't man-age access, we can't have that liability! Each house, each owner, is different. We simply can't be sure of our people in someone's home while the owners aren't there! What if some-thing happens?"

Do you follow this? Since home cleaning businesses believe they're incapable of knowing how to organize their time, they build a business based on lack of knowing and lack of control. They build a business based on estimates.

I once had a lady who owned a home cleaning business ask me, "What happens when we discover that a prospect is a hoarder? How can we deal with something so unexpected? How can we give proper service and stay on schedule?"

My first thought was that it's not being dealt with now. Few small business owners are able to give generously of their time. Ask anyone who's been trying to get a new housekeeper to come out to their home lately. It's chaos.

The solution is interest, attention, and analysis. Try detailing what you do at the beginning of a job, what you do in the middle, and what you do at the end. How long does each take? In the absence of such detailed, quantified standards, everything ends up being an estimate, and a poor estimate at that.

However, a home cleaning business organized around a system has time for proper attention. It's built right into the system.

Too many Technicians have grown accustomed to thinking in terms of estimates without thinking about what the term really means. Is it any wonder so few home cleaning businesses ever truly succeed? Why do so many continue to struggle year after year?

Enlightened business owners in the home cleaning industry, in contrast, banish the word *estimate* from their vocabulary. When it comes to estimating, *just say no!*

"But you can never be exact," others have told me for years. "Close, maybe. But never exact."

I have a simple answer to that: *You have to be.* You simply can't afford to be inexact. You can't accept inexactness in yourself or in your home cleaning business.

You can't go to work every day believing that your business, the work you do, and the commitments you make are all too complex and unpredictable to be exact. With a mindset like that, you're doomed to run a sloppy ship. A ship that will eventually sink and suck you down with it!

This is so easy to avoid. Sloppiness - in both thought and action - is the root cause of your frustrations.

The solution to those frustrations is clarity. Clarity gives you the ability to set a clear direction, which fuels the momentum you need to grow your business.

Clarity, direction, momentum - they all come from insisting on exactness.

But how do you create exactness in a hopelessly inexact world? The answer is this: You discover the exactness in your business by refusing to do any work that can't be controlled exactly.

The only other option is to analyze the market, determine where the opportunities are, and then organize your business to be the exact provider of the services you've chosen to offe .

It's really that simple. Two choices, and *only* two choices: (1) Evaluate your business and then limit yourself to the tasks you know you can do exactly, or (2) start all over by analyzing the market, identifying the key opportunities in that market, and building a business that operates exactly.

What you cannot do, what you must refuse to do, from this day forward, is to allow yourself to operate with an inexact mindset. It will lead you to ruin.

Which leads us inexorably back to the word I have been using through this book: *Systems*.

Who makes estimates? Only home cleaners who are unclear about exactly how to do the task in question. Only technicians whose experience has taught them that if something can go wrong, it will - and to them!

I'm not suggesting a systems solution will guarantee you always perform exactly as promised. But I am saying a systems solution will faithfully alert you when you're going off track and will do it before you have to pay the price for it.

In short, with a systems solution in place, your need to estimate will be a thing of the past, both because you have organized your business to anticipate mistakes, and because you have put into place the system to do something about those mistakes before they blow up.

There's this, too: To make a promise you intend to keep places a burden on you and your teams in the field to dig deeply into how you intend to keep it. Such a burden will transform your intentions and increase your attention to detail.

With the promise will come dedication. With dedication will come integrity. With integrity will come consistency. With consistency will come results you can count on. And results you can count on mean that you get exactly what you hoped for at the outset of your business: the true pride of ownership that every home cleaning business should demonstrate.

This brings us to the subject of *customers*. Who are they? Why do they come to you? How can you identify yours? And who *should* your customers be? But first, let's listen to what Russell has to say about *estimating*.

CHAPTER

14

Certainty is Invaluable

Russell O'Connell

"Trust is built with consistency."

—*Lincoln Chafee*

It might seem funny to headline a chapter about estimations "Certainty is Invaluable" since estimations are naturally the answer to a matter of *uncertainty*. But, as you will see, estimations should only be a tool for your own internal purposes—they should never be what you sell to customers.

As mentioned earlier, one of the things that people told us that they want, is consistency—no surprises. That means, what goes for today goes for tomorrow. Your customer should always know exactly what they'll be paying for your services. A set price. Not $200 one week and $300 the next.

Let's start by talking about pricing in a broader sense, though.

Almost to a "T" in the cleaning industry, the marketing and approach all revolves around low prices: "*cheap as chips*", "*we can do it cheaper*", "*we guarantee the lowest price*", "*great introductory discounts!*" and so on, and so forth. In other words, before prospective customers even get on the phone to them, these businesses have already devalued their brand.

Don't do it.

It's a proven fact: low prices erode trust—and high prices indicate that the product, for whatever reason, has a higher value, and that it's something you will be able to trust.

Now, our homes represent the single largest investment most of us will make financiall .

Will affluen clients open their doors and their wallets to the lowest-priced cleaners?

Will they trust that person to be in their home when they're not there?

They won't. Simple as that.

We know that we need to meet high expectations. And this means that your pricing needs to reflect what you as a business will need to deliver to those expectations.

Every time.

Without fail.

So, price accordingly.

You have to be so confident in your services that you can offer a price, not an estimate, which provides your business with the money it needs to provide your customer with a clean home to the standard you have set.

Before we even discuss estimating, though, you must consider your mindset about your pricing. There's an idea that "price" drives everything in the world, but the reality is, *value* drives it. And just what is that value to your clients?

There's value in knowing exactly what results they can expect and exactly how much they'll be paying for it.

There's value in being able to trust the people they let into their home (which might well contain a collection of sports cars and the odd Monet painting).

There is value in spending time with friends and family instead of cleaning.

For a moment, forget that you're in the home-cleaning industry. Like I said in an earlier chapter: *you're selling time to people whose time is worth a lot.*

Assume this mindset as you set your prices. Focus on the value that you provide, and you'll find that you can charge a lot more than you might have originally thought—and this resolves many of the problems that small home-cleaning businesses face.

You'll have the cash flow to purchase the proper materials to do the best job possible.

You'll have the income to hire and train better employees.

You'll have a high-quality clientele that will refer similar clients to you.

When you shift your mindset about pricing, you'll also begin to shift from a mindset of scarcity to one of abundance. Perhaps you haven't considered the value of this seemingly innocuous shift, but I assure you, it's very real.

When you see your clients as being abundant, and money as easy to make, you make better choices, you find better clientele, and you really do enjoy the work far more. Yes, this might seem a bit esoteric, and devilishly hard to get data on, but I've found, again and again, that it's true in all manner of business. And what's not to love about it!?

Finally, to the subject of this chapter: estimations. As I mentioned earlier, there's a place for estimations—but only as a tool for your internal purposes, and you should make sure that this tool is finely calibrated

In creating our Tri-colour™ Cleaning System, we collated reliable data on how long it takes for our average teams to accomplish each specific task to each of our specific standards. All we have to do now, is simply plug in the numbers to arrive at the total hours one might reasonably expect to spend cleaning a home. And we build that into our scheduling.

Precious few small cleaning companies collate and use this kind of data. In my experience, they rely on guesses and think in terms of "hours per house." Moreover, what most home cleaners would look at—room counts, square feet, and so on—are far from the most important factors. We can provide a firm *price*, not an estimate, by creating a relationship and understanding the client and their lives.

What does this mean in practice? For starters, much of what you need to know, you can learn through a short conversation on the phone. The prospect knows how many bedrooms and baths they have, they know where they live, and you know where your other clients are in relation to this particular address.

Depending on where in the world you live, you might even be able to pull up a floorplan of the residence, almost certainly the square footage. A quick search on social media could also tell you a great deal about the prospect.

Yet, time and again, busy Technicians put prospects off by proclaiming they'll have to come out and give an "estimate" on what a home-cleaning would cost, and of course, they're so "busy," they can't get out there until next week.

That's a crutch! What they really mean is they'll need to come by the house to begin bargaining with the prospect because they lack the confidence to give a specific pric

Let me tell you, if someone calls the offic and asks, "*I've only got a short time to speak, can you tell me what it would cost to have your team clean my home regularly?*", we can respond sincerely with, "Yes! Let us get a few details and we can absolutely get you the correct information."

An Ideal Client for MyHome is usually someone who doesn't have time in the first place. Why would we put them off or delay their inquiry by not being able to provide a price as soon as possible? We *will* give them a quote over the phone.

However, before we engage the customer, we will always go and visit them in their home.

We do this for three reasons.

The most important is to set expectation levels. Remember, good customer service is about meeting (or, better yet, *exceeding*) expectations, so it's imperative that the customer knows exactly what to expect. Without any set standard, you'll invariably find that you, as the owner of the business, the customers and your staff will have very different ideas of what constitutes "clean." That's why we take our time in personally explaining our Tri-colour™ Cleaning System. We also tell the prospect what to do if something goes wrong, how our satisfaction guarantee works, and how we use digital tools to conduct our services.

The second reason, which really is intertwined with the first, is to create a personal relationship. MyHome is a digital business supported by a lot of technology, but, at the end of the day, we're *in* the service industry, so we're also high-touch. Besides, we *enjoy* meeting and fostering relationships with new people—and we believe we're all the better for it.

The third reason is more practical: we have to verify that the details the prospects gave us over the phone are correct. And we have to go beyond the number of rooms, etc., to look at the prospects' lifestyle. Maybe they have a very nice house in a very nice suburb, but they also happen to be hoarders. Maybe they like entertaining and expect deep-cleans after every weekend? Maybe they have children and pets? Maybe they are simply very messy people?

You will be able to tell these things during a short visit. In fact, you'll know a lot even before you've done a tour of the house.

You'll know if it's a bad neighborhood when you get the address.

You'll know if the house is filthy when you walk in the door.

You'll know if it's safe for your teams almost instantly.

You can—and should—be able to meet a prospect, review their home, review your systems for achieving a clean home, and secure their business in one trip. Importantly, for every such trip, you have to assess as to whether that prospective customer really is a good fit for your business. If you find that they're not, be ready to explain why and walk away.

You cannot and must not accept customers who'd risk breaking your system.

In the vast majority of cases, however, you will have done your due diligence over the phone, and the customer is a good match. Still, going back to the high-touch aspect, don't just go through the motions here. Recognise how important this first visit is. It has virtually nothing to do with the price of the service—it has to do with the beginning of a relationship. Make sure that you create rapport. That's what it's all about at MyHome.

Most cleaning companies miss or simply do not take the above questions into account.

Then, since they don't know how much time will be required to clean the home, they insist on charging by the hour, sacrificing the consistency that builds trust and long-term relationships.

So, using the Tri-colour™ Cleaning System, we can—with great accuracy—predict how long it will take to clean a particular home. Does this mean that our teams never end up spending more time than expected? No, of course not. And that's fine—it s part of the art of estimating.

Think of the big picture. Setting fixed prices for your services is just like charging a fixed price for a hotel buffet lunch, where you have to allow for the fact that some guests will eat surprising amounts of food. Similarly, some of your customers' homes will take more time to clean than you'd accounted for. And since you're paying your employees by the hour, you might start stressing about this. Don't. Just stay focused on overall costs and profits, and set the individual KPIs that everyone in your company watches like a hawk.

Success is in the System™. Build it, maintain it—and trust it.

What about the fixed price then? What does it include

A true reflection of your costs

Remember Michael's Four Kinds of Money?

Your pricing—as we've now gone over—should reflect the *real* costs your home-cleaning company is incurring.

The vehicles.

The people.

The supplies.

The office overhead

E-v-e-r-y-t-h-i-n-g.

The hard truth is most Technicians can't—or won't—get clear on these numbers, and because of that, even their *estimates* feel wishy-washy: "we can *probably* do this for *approximately [X-Y]*".

What customer likes to hear that!?

Now, Technicians who do run the numbers on the real costs of doing business often get scared by the figure they arrive at. They look at what this or that cleaning company charges locally, and they soon forget their own in-house data and start second-guessing their pricing.

Their company is not yours.

Run your numbers, trust your systems and stand by your pricing—if you've set up your business well, it will be welcomed with open arms by the right clientele.

MyHome is not the highest-priced home-cleaning company in the areas we operate in, but we're not far behind. A different home-cleaning business (probably using subcontractors) could do an average job for a lot less than what my own company would quote.

But the customer would have to be there, because they have no idea just whom they're letting into their home.

They'd have to manage an invoice and remember to pay it.

They might get a great cleaning this week and a sloppy one next week, and then have to have the cleaners come back out because it wasn't up to par.

They'd never know exactly how much they'll be paying.

That's not making it easy for the customer. Making it easy for the customer is to do what we do at MyHome. Set fixed prices and have a system, such as our Tri-colour™ cleaning standards, in place to ensure consistent delivery of your services.

Again, trust is built with consistency. And remember: you'll be selling time to people whose time is worth a lot, and such people won't let you anywhere near their houses if there's a lack of trust.

Conversely, you'll be amazed at what you can charge when you give these people every reason to trust you 100%. Just like their time is invaluable, so is their peace of mind.

Rising Prices Aren't Hard Conversations

As I was writing this book, the world was going through a period of high inflation, and wages were constantly rising. Was this a cause for alarm? Certainly, for many small businesses, and surely the impact causes many home-cleaning companies some challenges… but for MyHome?

No. Not really.

Our system ensures that we build solid relationships with our clients, so the rise in our costs due to outside influences can be passed through to the customers with effective communication.

That's not to say that every minor increase in costs—due to fuel, due to wages, due to the economy—is passed through to our clients. Doing so would be bad business.

But we are *prepared* to have the conversation with every client that our pricing does require adjustment from time to time. And so should you be.

Time and again, I encounter Technicians who have *never* raised their prices. Year after year, their profits continue to decrease, because they haven't kept track of the individual types of money in the business—and they haven't built the strong customer relationships required to have challenging conversations.

And this is what we'll be talking about in the next two chapters: how to build strong relationships with the *right* customers.

Let's go back to Michael to dig into those customers.

CHAPTER

15

On the Subject of Customers

Michael E. Gerber

"Whether individuals or organizations, we follow those who lead not because we have to, but because we want to. We follow those who lead not for them, but for ourselves."

—Simon Sinek

When it comes to the business of home cleaning, the best definition of customers I've ever heard is this:

Customers: *very special people who drive us crazy.*

Does that work for you?

After all, it's a rare customer who shows any appreciation for what the technicians cleaning a home have to go through to do the job as promised. Don't they always think the price is too high? And don't they focus on problems, broken promises, and the mistakes they think you make, rather than all the ways you bend over backward to give them what they need?

Do you ever hear others in the field voice these complaints? More to the point, have you ever voiced them yourself? Well, you're not alone. I have yet to meet the owner of a home cleaning business who doesn't suffer from a strong case of customer confusion.

Customer confusion is about:

- What your customer really wants
- How to communicate effectively with your custome
- How to keep your customer truly happy
- How to deal with customer dissatisfaction
- Whom to call a customer

Confusion 1: What Your Customer Really Wants

Your customers aren't just people; they're very *specific* kinds of people. Let me share with you the six categories of customers as seen from The E-Myth marketing perspective: (1) tactile customers, (2) neutral customers, (3) withdrawal customers, (4) experimental customers, (5) transitional customers, and (6) traditional customers.

Your entire marketing strategy must be based on which type of customer you are dealing with. Each of the six customer types spends money on home cleaning services for very differ-ent, and identifiable, reasons. These are

- Tactile customers get their major gratification from inter acting with other people.

- Neutral customers get their major gratification fro interacting with inanimate objects (computers, cars, information).
- Withdrawal customers get their major gratification fro interacting with ideas (thoughts, concepts, stories).
- Experimental customers rationalize their buying decisions by perceiving that what they bought is new, revolutionary, and innovative.
- Transitional customers rationalize their buying decisions by perceiving that what they bought is dependable and reliable.
- Traditional customers rationalize their buying decisions by perceiving that what they bought is cost-effective, good deal, and worth the money.

In short:

- If your customer is tactile, you have to emphasize the *people* of your business.
- If your customer is neutral, you have to emphasize the *technology* of your business.
- If your customer is a withdrawal customer, you have to emphasize the *idea* of your business.
- If your customer is an experimental customer, you have to emphasize the *uniqueness* of your business.
- If your customer is transitional, you have to emphasize the *dependability* of your business.
- If your customer is traditional, you have to talk about the *financial competitiveness* of your business.

What your customers want is determined by who they are. Who they are is regularly demonstrated by what they do. Think about the customers with whom you do business. Ask yourself: In which of the categories would I place them? What do they do for a living?

If your customer is a mechanical engineer, for example, it's probably safe to assume he's a neutral customer. If another one of your customers is a cardiologist, she's probably tactile. Accountants tend to be traditional, and software engineers are often experimental.

Having an idea about which categories your customers may fall into is very helpful to figuring out what they want. Of course, there's no exact science to it, and human beings constantly defy stereotypes. So don't take my word for it. You'll want to make your own analysis of the customers you serve.

Confusion 2: How to Communicate Effectively with Your Customer

The next step in the customer satisfaction process is to decide how to magnify the characteristics of your business that are most likely to appeal to your preferred category of customer. That begins with what marketing people call your positioning strategy.

What do I mean by *positioning* your business? You position your business with words. A few well-chosen words to tell your customers exactly what they want to hear. In marketing lingo, those words are called your USP, or unique selling proposition.

For example, if you are targeting tactile customers (ones who love people), your USP could be: "Cozy Home Cleaners, where the comfort of people *really* counts!"

If you are targeting experimental customers (ones who love new, revolutionary things), your USP could be: "Smart Home Cleaning, where living on the edge is a way of life!" In other words, when they choose to schedule a home cleaning with you, they can count on both your services and equipment to utilize technology far more advanced than any other in the home cleaning business.

Is this starting to make sense? Do you see how the ordinary things most contractors do to get customers can be done in a significantly more effective wa

Once you understand the essential principles of marketing The E-Myth way, the strategies by which you attract customers can make an enormous differencein your market share.

Confusion 3: How to Keep Your Customer Happy

Let's say you've overcome the first two confusions. Great. Now how do you keep your customer happy?

Very simple ... *just keep your promise!* And make sure your customer *knows* you kept your promise every step of the way.

In short, giving your customers what they think they want is the key to keeping your customers (or anyone else, for that matter) really happy.

If your customers need to interact with people (high touch, tactile), make certain that they do.

If they need to interact with things (high tech, neutral), make certain that they do.

If they need to interact with ideas (in their head, withdrawal), make certain that they do.

And so forth.

Within The E-Myth, we call this your *customer fulfilment system.* It's the step-by-step process by which you do the task you've contracted to do and deliver what you've promised - on time, every time.

But what happens when your customers are *not* happy? What happens when you've done everything I've mentioned here and your customer is still dissatisfied

Confusion 4: How to Deal with Customer Dissatisfaction

If you have followed each step up to this point, customer dissatisfaction will be rare. But it can and will still occur - people are people, and some people will always find a way to be dissatisfied with something. Here's what to do about it:

- Always listen to what your customers are saying. And never interrupt while they're saying it.
- After you're sure you've heard all of your customer's complaint, make absolutely certain you understand what she said by phrasing a question such as: "Can I repeat what you've just told me, Ms. Harton, to make absolutely certain I understand you?"
- Secure your customer's acknowledgment that you have heard her complaint accurately.
- Apologize for whatever your customer thinks you did that dissatisfied her … even if you didn't do it
- After your customer has acknowledged your apology, ask her exactly what would make her happy.
- Repeat what your customer told you would make her happy, and get her acknowledgement that you have heard correctly.
- If at all possible, give your customer exactly what she has asked for.

You may be thinking, "But what if my customer wants something totally impossible?" Don't worry. If you've followed my recommendations to the letter, what your customer asks for will seldom seem unreasonable.

Confusion 5: Whom to Call a Customer

At this stage, it's important to ask yourself some questions about the kind of customers you hope to attract to your business:

- Which types of customers would you most like to do business with?
- Where do you see your real market opportunities?
- Who would you like to work with, provide services to, and position your business for?

In short, *it's all up to you.* No mystery. No magic. Just a systematic process for shaping your company's future. But you must have the passion to pursue the process. And you must be absolutely clear about every aspect of it.

Until you know your customers as well as you know yourself.

Until all your complaints about customers are a thing of the past.

Until you accept the undeniable fact that customer acquisition and customer satisfaction are more science than art.

But unless you're willing to grow your business, you better not follow any of these recommendations. Because if you do what I'm suggesting, it's going to grow.

This brings us to the subject of growth. But first, let's see what our own home cleaning entrepreneur has to say about *customers.*

CHAPTER

16

System Success is Customer Success

Russell O'Connell

"Build it, and they will come."

—Famous misquote from **Field of Dreams** (the actual quote is "if you build it, he will come")

We seem to be on a roll with the movie quotes, don't we? Here's one more from Randal Graves in the movie Clerks, "*This job would be great if it wasn't for the [expletive] customers!*"

And let's wheel out another old chestnut whilst we're at it: the saying, "the customer is always right."

The first quote is simply not true for all too many businesses. Building 'it' simply doesn't cut it. 'It' needs to be appealing, 'it' needs to be desirable, and people need to be persuaded to come to 'it.' A more realistic quote, for a business, should be, "*Design it right, build it right, sell it right and they will come.*" Think Steve Jobs and Apple — a beautifully designed and highly desirable product sold with the incredible persuasiveness and passion of Steve Jobs.

The second quote we opened the chapter with, sadly, is all too true — there ARE customers out there who are downright impossible to deal with. But, as you'll see, in your business, you will never be able to blame them for that. If some of your customers turn out to be impossible to deal with, that's a sign that your system is broken. We'll get back to that shortly.

And as for that classic saying "the customer is aways right", that's simply and plainly wrong. The customer ISN'T always right!

However, "the *right* customer is always *right*" — and this, too, comes back to your system, and whom it's built for.

So, here we are, quickly digressing to talk about systems in a chapter that's supposed to be about customers.

Why?

Because you probably need to reframe your thinking around customers. Have a think about what they currently represent to you. Do you think of the customer as a source of income? As someone whose home you clean? As someone who spreads word about your stellar services, so that you can get more business?

Sure, your customer can, and should be, all of these things. But there's another characteristic that underpins everything else. Something that is absolutely critical to your success.

Remember an earlier subheading, "*Definitions create the system*"? We were talking about standards then. Standards, i.e., known entities, are the cogs in your system. Standards for your cleaning, as defined by MyHome's Tri-colour™ Cleaning System, for example.

Standards for your fixed prices. Standards for your employment conditions, for your branded vehicles, for your uniforms—standards for every last aspect of your how, right down to the way you fold cleaning cloths.

And guess what! Your customers should be known entities, too.

This might sound harsh—and please don't think for a second that I treat people as mere numbers—but from a systems point of view, think of your customers as standardized units. Without standardized units, without definitions, your system will break.

And, it bears repeating: *Success is in the System™*.

The characteristic I mentioned earlier is consequently this: your customers must meet a specific criterion which means that they will 'fit' and work with your system

You create a system that's a perfect fit for your Ideal Customers, and they will make the cogs and gears in your "little money machine" spin flawlessl .

Build it and they will come? Or…

"*Design it right, build it right, sell it right and they will come.*"

Ergo, you need to define your Ideal Customer as precisely as possible.

Exactly who is your ideal customer?

Remember what I said in an earlier chapter: it's best not to make too many assumptions about what the customer appreciates most. In systems-based thinking, guesses and estimates are your foes. Facts and strict standards are your friends. So, don't just paint a picture of an imagined Ideal Customer. The Ideal Customers are already out there—go and talk to them!

The first thing I did on taking over MyHome in the UK, was to conduct hundreds of interviews with the existing customers. We asked lots of questions and collated the answers. And much to our surprise, we soon found that a clean home wasn't necessarily at the top of their wish list.

How did we identify this?

Simple. *We asked them what their concerns were!*

What was on their mind when choosing a cleaner. And we asked what mattered, really mattered, to them. We wanted to know what the 'conversation in their head with themselves' was as they thought about what they really wanted and who to choose. What were their reservations, fears and frustrations about and with people like us – cleaners and cleaning businesses.

By the way, our 'them' wasn't everyone who said they wanted a cleaner, our 'them' were people living in the homes, the areas and from the demographic that we wanted as customers---in other words, the 'right' customers… for us.

When we asked, they told us.

And when we analysed all the concerns that the customers expressed to us during these interviews, there were three that came through over and over again.

Here's what they said…

"I need to know what I am going to get". We discovered that our 'ideal' customer valued CONSISTENTCY. Not a great clean just the first time, not sometimes, not even most times---they valued the same (high) standard of cleaning EVERY time.

They also told us that they needed to have complete trust and confidence in the cleaners they chose---that they could trust them in their home and with their keys, around their pets and with their credit card details. It was absolutely clear that they valued security, confidentiality and honesty---a company they could depend on.

And they said they valued a high standard of cleaning. Customers wanted a beautifully clean home and they wanted to be sure that they were going to get what they expected---a consistently HIGH standard of service.

So, we decided to design and build our company around three key promises— Care, Dependability, and Expertise. And we made sure to give our customers reasons to believe that we would deliver on these promises:

1 Care

Customer concern: "*How do I know these people cleaning my home share my belief in what clean really is, and what a home cleaning will cost every fortnight?*"
Promise: Specific standards for everything— you will know exactly what to expect when you choose MyHome.

Reasons to believe:

- Standardised cleaning as set out with the Tri-colour™ system
- Standardised (fixed) pric
- Standardised staffing—trained full-time employees onl no subcontractors
- Standardised, professional equipment
- Standardised, GECA-certified cleaning product
- Standardised payment processes

All of these standards are high and well defined MyHome has a proven record of consistently delivering first class service.

#2 Dependability

Customer concern: "*I won't know who is in my home, if they've got insurance, if they're trustworthy with my keys, my pets, my belongings, or even my credit card information!*"
Promise: Dependability—with MyHome, you'll know that your home is in safe hands for your peace of mind.

Reasons to believe:

- MyHome vet all staff prior to hiring
- MyHome only hire full-time employees, no subcontractors.
- Your home is always serviced by a two-person team.
- MyHome is fully insured.
- Secure payment system.
- Strict procedures for key management with possession log and secure storage (fun fact: MyHome s head office at a former financial institution, so we keep all custome keys in an actual bank vault it s like Fort Knox!).
- Established for over 15 years, MyHome has thousands of satisfied, discerning customers

#3 Expertise

Customer concern: "*I don't know what will happen if I'm not happy with the service.*"
Promise: Satisfaction—guaranteed
Reason to believe:

- The MyHome satisfaction guarantee—if you're not happy, we'll come back and rectify the issue free of charge.
- MyHome customer service is readily available during all office hours—call our office, and you'll get to tal a real human being who will address your concern right away.

These promises are expressed in the details of our 'How'—our Tri-colour™ Cleaning System, our digital platforms and applications, our branded vehicles and uniforms. Every last detail that forms part of the customer experience and makes us different from the competition

Keep in mind: if you don't clearly distinguish your home-cleaning company from others, prospect customers will only ever be able to evaluate your service based on price—and we know where that leads.

Down to rock bottom.

Now, finding out what customers actually want from you is a great start. But as we touched on earlier, you also have to ask yourself who, of all these people, who do you actually want as your customers. Exactly who should you build your system for? Who should you include? And who should you exclude?

Perhaps you've heard of Pareto's Principle, also known as the 80/20 Rule?

Eighty percent of your problems come from just twenty percent of your clients. While the 20% of your potential market will be in your 'sweet spot', your ideal customers.

By knowing exactly who your ideal twenty percenters are, you'll be able to target, attract and keep them with real precision.

This principle is surprisingly useful in business. But remember: everything is relative. With a curated customer base of people who fit into your system, your problems will be relatively small. So, it's crucial to pay attention to detail when defining your Ideal Custome .

Don't just listen to what people say in focus group interviews—think about what it means. It's a bit like being a psychotherapist. People will give you a lot of details about their lives—it's up to you to identify their innermost needs and motivations.

What I found was that our "ideal" customer lived in a very specific geographic area, was value-conscious rather than price-conscious—they were time-poor, with professional careers and families to care for.

They told me they wanted security; they wanted to know who was going to be in their home.

They wanted the consistency that a clearly defined cleaning system could provide them on a regular basis, delivered by well-trained team members, not subcontractors. Importantly, they understood the value of a cleaning system, they had realistic expectations, and they would be happy to entrust us with the keys to their home and pay via credit card.

These are the customers you want—the RIGHT customers.

So, be selective.

Don't be surprised if you find yourself turning down a lot of potential customers. That's okay. You're not in business to have the maximum number of customers. Remember, it's about having a business that follows a proven system—and that has to be populated by the right customers.

Case in point: when I took over MyHome from Unilever in the UK, they had a roster of nearly 2,000 clients—and they were losing tens of thousands of pounds a week. Having identified the Ideal Customer, I shrunk that roster down to 750 customers—*the right customers*—and within less than three months, the business was generating a profit

Knowing who is our Ideal Customer allowed us to develop the marketing materials and the systems that catered to these ideal clients' needs—and reinforced to them that MyHome was unique among home-cleaning businesses.

Even now, long after we've built out MyHome and I've spoken with literally thousands of prospects and customers over the years, the fact we've continued to be keenly aware of whom we were built to serve pays off handsomely. As we've mentioned previously, this focus on the 'right' customer must be a core tenet of your home-cleaning business, just as it is in MyHome; after all, "Winning Customers" is one of our Six Pillars. The creation of a system to do this work allows us to easily do the following—again, not relying on "people", but on systems run by people:

- We know where to focus our marketing efforts
- We know the core issues our Ideal Customers care about.
- We know exactly what to say to attract and persuade our Ideal Customers.
- We focus strictly on a specific demographic and sta exclusively in that "sweet spot."
- The systems we've developed and use are designed to take care of one specific client base – our Idea Customers.
- Our systems eliminate the cash-flow issues even ou Ideal Customers could inadvertently create.
- The processes we have created, based on the Tricolour™ Cleaning System, dramatically reduce the odds of a "bad" customer experience.

But no matter how well you prepare for it, clients are, ultimately, people, and Michael's observation from earlier in the book still stands: people are unmanageable!

Here's a hint: since you can't manage them, you can at least make sure you're dealing with nice people. Why have angry, spiteful customers? Life is too short—find and keep the ones who are pleasant to deal with, and let your systems do the rest.

This leads us to the next subject: How to create strong customer relationships.

When you gain clarity on what your customer really wants, it becomes far easier to communicate with them—thereby building solid relationships. This is the essence of good customer relationships: to be clear in setting expectations and then to meet, or, better yet, exceed the customers' expectations in delivering your services.

Of course, any relationship is a two-way street. Just like customers have to be clear on what they can expect from you, they have to be clear on what you expect from them. You have to explain the rules of the game. For example, the customer needs to understand that you have to have a window of time for when you can clean their homes, and that cancelling at the last minute will throw out the scheduling of your full-time staff

All of the above is part of the conversation when we go out to see prospect customers in their homes. Remember the quote from an earlier chapter: "Trust is built on consistency?" What we're doing here is defining what constitutes that consistency--- both in terms of what customers should expect from us and what we should expect from customers.

The net result is mutual respect, and there's no better starting point for a strong customer relationship.

Understand Your Area of Influence

Just because you've got a cleaning business in Melbourne, Atlanta, or London doesn't mean you should take ownership of the entire city. For example, if every client you have lies to the west of your home or office you should be wary of taking on a new client half an hour *east* of you.

That would mean a round trip of a full hour, and in MyHome's case, that equals two manhours, since we only operate teams of two. Add the total costs for fuel and vehicle maintenance, and you'll start seeing that prospect new customer in a new light.

But what if one of your team members happens to live near that faraway prospect customer? Then it's pretty tempting to think, "team member so-and-so will clean that customer's home on their way to work—we'll take the job!" Don't. If anything in your system is dependent on one individual employee, then you've got a single point of failure.

Also, ask yourself this, if you WERE to take on such a customer, how many ideal customers would your team be driving past on their way to that job? Chances are, if you've got one client in a neighbourhood, you've got the potential for a lot of other clients right there.

Bottom line: quit selling in cities, start selling in neighbourhoods.

Imagine a nice, tight cluster of clients all on one street! You don't need many of those to run an incredibly profitable home-cleaning company.

You might also want to reframe how you think about customers. They're not just individual customer of yours who live in a defined geographical area. They're members of the local community, and your business should be central to this community.

I'll give you an example. Some years ago, a businessman by the name of Dara took over a failing coffee shop close to our offices and renamed it Sanctuary & C

I watched with interest to see what he'd make of it. I knew that he'd be competing with another coffee shop that's in a better location. But, in short order, his place was packed with customers whilst the competitor's business dwindled. How could this be? His coffee was much the same as theirs, and his location wasn't nearly as attractive.

The difference lay in that he had spent time planning, creating a system that worked for him, so that he could work on rather than in his business. In practice this means that he can spend time on the floor talking to his customers. He knows everyone by name, he's got everyone's confidence—he s made himself part of people's inner circles. No wonder that people flock to his café. They could have gone to a fancier location for the same coffee, but they come to see Dara, to connect with someone and feel part of the community.

Take a page from his book. Create a business that works for you, so that you will have the time and energy to get involved with your local community. Support other local businesses and charities and don't shy away from promoting or having a presence at community events. It doesn't only pay dividends in your bottom line—it is and feels meaningful. You become part of something bigger than yourself, making other people's lives better. And that is, in itself, a great driving force to move onward and upward.

Keep in mind that your business should be about enjoying life!

How to Deal with Customer Dissatisfaction

Mistakes will happen. There will be complaints. You can't avoid that. But you can choose how to react to those mistakes and complaints—and this can set your company apart from all others.

At MyHome, we've got a satisfaction guarantee. If we don't deliver on our promises, we'll go back to the customer's home and sort it out, without quibbles and free of charge.

99.9% of the time, this fixes the issue for the customer, and we're back in their good graces. Then we naturally make sure to address how the mistake was allowed to occur in the first place. It s an opportunity to strengthen our systems.

Was there a scheduling challenge? Did we ask too much of the team that cleaned the home? Did a team member simply forget to clean a particular room?

This is another area where it really helps to build your business on strong customer relationships. When you have a solid track record with a customer, they are much more understanding. They know your high standards, and as long as you're quick to remedy a mistake, all is forgiven. You also know that they're likely to stay with you for a long time, so you can weigh the costs of free-of-charge cleans against the lifetime value of the customers.

Ultimately, my experience is that the easiest solution is to simply address the issue, clean the home, or at least the problem area, free of charge and move on. Don't overthink it, don't view complaints as an attack, but as an opportunity to learn and adjust your system.

Contrast this with what it's like to handle complaints arising from odd jobs, where there's no relationship. There's a high risk that you'll never convert that customer into a regular, so you might never recoup the costs of a free-of-charge clean. What's more, your brand will still be impacted by their negative experience, and you can't even learn from your mistake to improve on your system—because you don't have any.

Of course, we candidly review our customers, too. Are they picky? Is there a history with the client and the team that is in the home?

Know this: you cannot please everyone.

Even when you've set your systems up to perfection and vetted your prospect clients before accepting their business, you're going to have people who don't appreciate your services. That's ok. Just make sure that you deliver on your promises and be ready to walk away if that's still not to the customer's liking. Bending to such customers' will would mean breaking your system—and we know what happens then.

Again, don't overthink things. If this happens, you didn't do anything wrong—your service simply wasn't for that particular customer.

Bear this in mind when you read reviews of your business online. Don't be discouraged by some negative comments—they're par for the course. Take the Harry Potter franchise for example. It's got *thousands* of bad reviews, yet, taken as a whole, the good far outweigh the bad—and the profits of Harry Potter's "little money machine" are astronomical.

So, sure, read all reviews, learn what there's to learn and refine your systems accordingly. But acknowledge that your business isn't for everyone. That's the way it's supposed to be.

Now, speaking of reviews, some are more important than others. Going back to Pareto's Principle, the 80/20 rule, we've identified the top 20 percent of our customers and made it our mission to truly wow them.

Our approach actually extends beyond customers to embrace all potential brand advocates—community leaders, other local businesspeople and so on. We take our time to foster particularly close relationships with these people. For customers, it might mean paying special attention in vetting the teams who clean their homes and making regular courtesy calls, and no matter whether they're a customer or not, we congratulate them on their birthdays, send them personal holiday greetings and so on. At MyHome, these 20% become influencers who generate a huge volume of referrals and goodwill.

So, in summary, know whom you serve and build your business systems around them. Ultimately, they're the key to our next chapters, where Michael and I discuss growth.

CHAPTER

17

On the Subject of Growth

Michael E. Gerber

"All organizations are hierarchical. At each level people serve under those above them. An organization is therefore a structured institution. If it is not structured, it is a mob. Mobs do not get things done, they destroy things."

—Theodore Levitt, Marketing for Business Growth

The rule of business growth says that every company, like every child, is destined to grow.

Needs to grow.

Is determined to grow.

Once you've created your home cleaning business, once you've shaped the idea of it, the most natural thing for it to do is to ... *grow*! And if you stop it from growing, it will die.

Once a person has started a company, it's his or her job to help it grow. To nurture it and support it in every way. To infuse it with:

- Purpose
- Passion
- Will
- Belief
- Personality
- Method

As your business grows, it naturally changes. And as it changes from a small business to something much bigger, you will begin to feel out of control. News flash: That's because you *are* out of control.

Your business *has* exceeded your know-how, sprinted right past you, and now it's taunting you to keep up. That leaves you two choices: Grow as big as your business demands you grow, or try to hold your business at its present level - at the level you feel most comfortable.

The sad fact is that most home cleaning businesses simply stay small. The owner tries to keep it that way, securely within their comfort zone. Doing what they know how to do, what they feel most comfortable doing. It's called playing it safe.

But as the business grows, the number, scale, and complexity of tasks will grow, too, until they threaten to overwhelm the very person who started it. More people are needed. More space. More money. Everything seems to be happening at the same time. A hundred balls are in the air at once.

As I've said throughout this book: Most small business owners are not entrepreneurs. They aren't true businesspeople at all, but technicians suffering from an entrepreneurial seizure. Their philosophy of coping with the workload can be summarized as "just do it," rather than figuring out how to get it done through other people using innovative systems to produce consistent results.

Given most technician's inclination to be the master juggler in their business, it's not surprising that as complexity increases, as work expands beyond their ability to do it, as money becomes more elusive, they are just holding on, desperately juggling more and more balls. In the end, most collapse under the strain.

You can't expect your business to stand still. You can't expect your business to stay small. A company that stays small and depends on you to do everything isn't a company - it's a *job*!

Yes, just like your children, your business must be allowed to grow, to flourish, to change, to become more than it is. In this way, it will match your vision. And you know all about vision, right? You better. It's what you do best!

Do you feel the excitement? You should. After all, you know what your business *is* but not what it *can be*.

It's either going to grow or die. The choice is yours, but it is a choice that must be made. If you sit back and wait for change to overtake you, you will always have to answer "no" to this question: *Are you ready?*

That brings us to the subject of *change*. But first, let's see what Russell has to say about *growth*.

CHAPTER 18

Making Growth Part of Your Business DNA

Russell O'Connell

"The journey of a thousand miles begins with a single step."

— *Lao Tzu*

Look carefully at the quote above. Many people interpret it on a fairly superficial level. To them, it simply means something like, "don't be disheartened by the monumental task ahead—you simply have to *dare* to start your journey". But there's so much more wisdom in what Lao said.

Let's unpack it.

If you're a parent, chances are that you remember the very first steps your child or children took. It was something of real significance—a cause for celebration. But why? What was it that made it such an awesome event? Because it wasn't about that singular occurrence. It was because it was a sign of growth, a promise of great things ahead.

You might not have been aware of it at the time, but there would have been several concepts that you took ownership of at that moment, and these are crucial to growth.

One such concept is repeatability. You knew that those first steps weren't chance events and that the greatness lay in the fact that your child was developing a way to make this a repeatable action, of turning the art of walking into second nature.

Another concept is incrementality. You accepted the fact that your toddler was only starting out and wasn't about to beat Usain Bolt in a 100m dash. You knew that you could expect your child to *gradually* learn to walk before even attempting a run.

Yet another concept is potentiality. Learning to walk is great thing in its own right, but the real point is in everything else that it enables you to do (although, initially, this might mostly consist of clearing out the bottom part of every bookshelf or chasing siblings and family pets around the house).

Perhaps most obvious is the concept of achievement. For your toddler, those first steps are a big win. A milestone to be celebrated.

In a similar fashion—and for the same reasons—you will remember and celebrate a great many other milestones in your child's life.

The same principles are true for your home-cleaning business, and that's truly a beautiful thing, because there are plenty of other industries where the market is already more or less saturated, where you can be among the very best and still struggle to survive.

No matter where you are in the world, there are really no outside blockers to the growth of your home-cleaning business.

Put out a flier with your name and number and the phone *will* ring.

As mentioned earlier, this is why you'll find so many technicians in the home-cleaning industry. They know that it's a surefire way of quickly making some money on their own. But, in short order, they'll find themselves overwhelmed with work—they will collapse under the weight of their own growth and either give up or retreat to a level that they can manage, toiling away year after year without making any real progress.

Of course, this also why you, the proactive entrepreneur, have such a golden opportunity in the home-cleaning industry. Most of the time, you'll be competing with technicians who are completely reactive, not having any system to manage growth and scale their businesses.

Just to make sure that we're on the same page, though, let's pause for a second and define what growth *should* mean in your business. Is it doing more? Is it growing your customer base? Is it growing your income?

It's none of those things alone—and, as far as you as a business owner are concerned, it certainly should NOT be doing more. *Getting more done*, yes. But not *doing more*. Your systems should enable you to get more done without your having to get any busier.

However, building a system to ensure that you won't have to do more to get more done does take time—and building a system that can scale to 100 employees and beyond is surely more challenging than building a system that can cope with 20.

This brings us to an important question: what's your goal? In the home-cleaning business, the sky really is the limit, but big goals do mean that you have to put more time and energy into building scalable systems. You'll want to strike a good balance.

My advice: don't just set yourself the goal of making X amount of money in Y time. A figure is just a figure—what ultimately matters is what you want to achieve in life. So, instead of thinking about money alone, think about the lifestyle that you want and work backward from that.

There are financial aspects in this, of course—there are plenty of things that require considerable amounts of money. Maybe you want a certain size house in a certain neighbourhood. Maybe you want to send your children to the most prestigious schools. Maybe you want to invest in great art pieces. Maybe you want a boat, a sportscar or a holiday home on the beach.

But don't just paint yourself a picture of a life in luxury. Have a really good think about what actually makes you and your family happy. There are plenty of wealthy people who are constantly stressed out and never able to truly enjoy what their money can buy them. Which brings us to the other aspect: your lifestyle as you build your business.

Do you want to have a four-day workweek? Do you want to finish work in time to pick up your kids from school every day? Do you want to be able to go on extended family holidays without having to worry about your business whilst you're away?

At MyHome, we do this exercise with our prospect franchise partners from the onset, before we commit to going into business together. We explore questions like: What are their expectations for growth? For their own quality of life? For top-line sales? For bottom-line profits? For equity? What does their weekend look like, any given month? Where will they go on holiday this year?

It's only when you begin to see things in a larger sense of how it all fits together and what is truly important to you that you can set reliable goals.

Factor all these things in. *Do* arrive at that figure (and don't be shy—if your idea of a happy life requires lots of money, it's there for the taking), but also consider your work-life balance.

And be realistic.

Look at how much salary you need to draw every week. How many clients you'd need at different stages of your growth journey. And don't aim for explosive growth. Plan for incremental growth, and be ready to deal with the hurdles that will inevitably come your way—what we refer to as "definable points." Let's talk about them next, because they will be upon you before you know it!

Definable Points

The first "definable point" is usually where you, as a Company of One, run out of time, but as your business grows, you'll come again and again to others. Ironically, nearly every one of these definable points are a version of the same problem. You or your team physically cannot clean another home, because there simply isn't time in your week! It's easiest to view these as a fork in the road your business is on, and the reality is, each time you get to another one of these points, you've got three choices: stay where you are, begin to delegate and manage, or find higher-paying customers.

For 95% or more of home-cleaning companies, the Technician who began the company is stuck at the first defi -able point, but the beauty of growth is that once you understand how to proceed past one point, you fundamentally understand how to deal with every one in the future. With that in mind, let's work through the first stage of growth, because you MUST have your business philosophy correct, or growth will always be elusive.

So, here we are: you've opened your home-cleaning business, things are going great, you're busy, busy, busy, and your clients love the work you do… but your Sunday is filled with administrative work, you're frankly exhausted, and while the money is "good" you feel you could be doing far better. Welcome to the fork in the road!

Should you hire someone?

Should you try to find higher-paying clients

Should you simply decide "this is enough" and stay static?

Here's my answer: at every definable point, *the solution is a system*. Now, that system might be one designed elsewhere—an app that handles your scheduling, a payment processing software that handles invoicing, or an employee that fills a specific role for your company and has a manual of operations on how to do so.

While the solution is to lean heavily into your systems (or create them), it's critical to understand that immediately *after* you take action on a definable point, you will more than likely see a dip in your cash flo . Don't fall into the trap of seeing this as a negative result of your new system—see it as an opportunity to address your pricing long term.

You, as the entrepreneur, should be prepared to, if necessary, take a smaller percentage of the profit in your company in the short term, in return for far higher sales and the opportunity to build real equity in your business in the future.

Accepting That Growth Will Mean Further Investment

A critical definable point, one that you will come up against again and again, is when you yourself get too busy to work *on* the business rather than *in* it. Most small business owners don't appreciate the significance of this. They cling to the old idea of simply doing everything themselves, giving their own time no monetary value.

Here's a reminder: you are not just a worker bee in a cleaning company, you're a founder. You're a creator. *Your time matters*, even if you can't yet see it. While your company is still small, you must learn to value your time, especially if you wear a lot of hats in your home-cleaning company, which is nearly impossible to avoid.

You're Payroll now, you'll be HR in an hour. After lunch, you'll be the Sales department, then at 3:00 p.m., you might "clock in" to clean a home.

Since you're so "busy," you're probably going to hate me for this next suggestion: learn what each of those positions pays in the real world—and, as you do them in your home-leaning business, keep tabs. Track the hours. Document the expenses. Know the real costs of your inexperience in terms of the time it takes you and the costs of that time, and write down exactly how you do the jobs in those positions.

Now, the answers provided by your analyses will not be perfect, but they will allow you to project and budget—two things most small home-cleaning businesses never do. You'll have a baseline for the answer every Technician on the planet has asked when confronted with growth: "*What's THIS going to cost me?*"

Inevitably, a definable point IS going to cost money. It might be a SaaS (software as a service), it might be more hourly team members, it might be a layer of management, or, at higher levels, an IPO or the creation of a leadership team.

It's ALL going to cost you, and most Technicians despise that idea.

By contrast, Entrepreneurs embrace the costs of adding more overhead—provided that, in the long term, these overheads will *increase profit* .

Overheads are part and parcel of systems-based solutions, which in turn are about creating predictable revenue and organic growth. Without substantial overheads, you will have no substantial system—and without a substantial, well-calibrated system, you have little to no equity.

Think again about McDonald's little money machine. What is it really that their franchisees are paying for? They're actually buying an extremely well-defined set of overheads. Overheads that Ray Croc chose to bet on after having gone through exactly the type of exercise described above—analysing and documenting every last second and cost of doing business. And since he was rather the perfectionist, that proved to be a winning bet. You could say that McDonald's *overheads* are today valued at over $209 *billion* (McDonald's market cap as of this writing).

MyHome have taken the same approach in the home-cleaning industry. We've defined what "clean" means. We've defined just whom we should serve. We've defined how to teach novice people to clean. Much like McDonald's, we've set standards for nigh-on every last detail in our business. And we know the customer acquisition costs, the costs of our vehicles and supplies and everything else—the main fluctuating cost is our marketing. So, we can with great accuracy predict and plan for every definable point ahead

But this naturally requires a lot of work—do you have to do all of it in one fell swoop? No! Again, work incrementally, identifying and planning in advance to overcome the next definable point in your business. You need only stay a few steps ahead, and it would be foolhardy for you to start by designing an app as robust as what we use at MyHome, which cost me a fortune to create, but which will support our team and franchise partners for decades to come.

Think back on the quote at the start of this chapter: "The journey of a thousand miles begins with a single step." Develop your systems like this. Step by step.

It's not *that* hard to create a training program that goes beyond "just watch what I do".

It's not all too difficul to spend an hour in the evening becoming clear on whose home you wish to clean, and what *they* really desire.

It's even perfectly possible for you to, right now, define the exact steps you take to achieve the "clean" standard that your business advertises.

In most cases, we're literally talking about investing less than an hour a day. Thus, it's a matter of personal discipline. Much like physical training. It really doesn't require very much time—but the benefits are invaluable

One last thought on your growth journey: be kind to yourself. It's devilishly hard to open a business today and wait five years for a reward, so set goals incrementall .

If your goal is to build a seven-figure business, that doesn't happen overnight. Set that goal, but have smaller monthly, quarterly or annual goals to reward yourself for the pace you're setting. For your mental health as a leader, you need to be able to celebrate wins.

Remember to stay grounded, though—you must never let the ambition for growth consume you. Having that happen would mean losing your happiness, and what's the point of it all then!?

Growth should never control you.

You should control growth.

On that note, let's talk about developing that winning mindset.

Here's Michael.

CHAPTER 19

On the Subject of Change

Michael E. Gerber

"Our Leaders of today need the philosophy of the past, paired with the scientific knowledge and technology of tomorrow.

—Anders Indset

So your home cleaning company is growing. That means, of course, that it's also *changing.* Which means it's driving you and everyone in your life crazy.

That's because, to most people, change is a diabolical thing. Tell most people they've got to change, and their first instinct is to crawl directly into a hole. Nothing threatens their existence more than change. Nothing cements their resistance more than change. Nothing!

Yet for more than forty years, that's exactly what I've been proposing to small business owners: the need to change. Not for the sake of change itself, but for the sake of their lives.

I've talked to countless business owners whose hopes weren't being realized through their business; whose lives were consumed by work; who slaved increasingly longer hours for decreasing pay; whose dissatisfaction grew as their enjoyment shriveled; whose business had become the worst job in the world; whose money was out of control; whose employees were a source of never-ending hassles, just like their customers, their bank, and, increasingly, even their family.

More and more, these men and women spent their time alone, dreading the unknown and anxious about the future. And even when they were with people, they didn't know how to relax. Their mind was always on the job. They were distracted by work, by the thought of work. By the fear of falling behind.

And yet, when confronted with their condition and offered an alternative, most of the same business owners strenuously resisted it. They assumed that if there were a better way of doing business, they already would have figured it out. They derived comfort from knowing what they believed they already knew. They accepted the limitations of being in the home cleaning industry; or the truth about people; or the limitations of what they could expect from their customers, their employees, their subcontractors, their bankers - even their family and friends.

In short, most of the technicians I've met over the years would rather live with the frustrations they already have than risk enduring new frustrations.

Isn't that true of most people you know? Rather than opening up to the infinite number of possibilities life offers, they prefer to shut their lives down to respectable limits. After all, isn't that the most reasonable way to live?

I think not. I think we must learn to let go. I think that if you fail to embrace change, it will inevitably destroy you.

Conversely, by opening yourself to change, you give your home cleaning business the opportunity to get the most from your talents.

Let me share with you an original way to think about change, about life, about who we are and what we do. About the stunning notion of expansion and contraction.

Contraction versus Expansion

"Our salvation," a wise man once said, "is to allow." That is, to be open, to let go of our beliefs, to change. Only then can we move from a point of view to a viewing point.

That wise man was Thaddeus Golas, the author of a small, powerful book entitled *The Lazy Man's Guide to Enlightenment* (Seed Center, 1971).

Among the many inspirational things he had to say was this compelling idea:

> *The basic function of each being is expanding and contracting. Expanded beings are permeative; contracted beings are dense and impermeative. Therefore each of us, alone or in combination, may appear as space, energy, or mass, depending on the ratio of expansion to contraction chosen, and what kind of vibrations each of us expresses by alternating expansion and contraction. Each being controls his or her own vibrations.*

In other words, Golas tells us that the entire mystery of life can be summed up in two words: *expansion* and *contraction.* He goes on to say:

> *We experience expansion as awareness, comprehension, understanding, or whatever we wish to call it.*

When we are completely expanded, we have a feeling of total awareness, of being one with all life.

At that level we have no resistance to any vibrations or interactions of other beings. It is timeless bliss, with unlimited choice of consciousness, perception, and feeling.

When a (human) being is totally contracted, he is a mass particle, completely imploded.

To the degree that he is contracted, a being is unable to be in the same space with others, so the contraction is felt as fear, pain, unconsciousness, ignorance, hatred, evil, and a whole host of strange feelings.

At an extreme (of contraction, a human being) has the feeling of being completely insane, of resisting everyone and everything, of being unable to choose the content of his consciousness.

Of course, these are just the feelings appropriate to mass vibration levels, and he can get out of them at any time by expanding, by letting go of all resistance to what he thinks, sees, or feels.

Stay with me here. Because what Golas says is profoundly important. When you're feeling oppressed, overwhelmed, exhausted by more than you can control - contracted, as Golas puts it - you can change your state to one of expansion.

According to Golas, the more contracted we are, the more threatened we are by change; the more expanded we are, the more open we are to change.

In our most enlightened - that is, open - state, change is as welcome as non-change. Everything is perceived as a part of ourselves. There is no inside or outside. Everything is one thing. Our sense of isolation is transformed to a feeling of ease, of light, of joyful relationship with everything.

As infants, we didn't even think of change in the same way, because we lived those first days in an unthreatened state. Insensitive to the threat of loss, most young children are only aware of *what is*. Change is simply another form of *what is*. Change just *is*.

However, when we are in our most contracted - that is, closed - state, change is the most extreme threat. If the known is what I have, then the unknown must be what threatens to take away what I have. Change, then, is the unknown. And the unknown is fear. It's like being between trapezes.

- To the fearful, change is threatening because things may get worse.
- To the hopeful, change is encouraging because things may get better.
- To the confident, change is inspiring because the chal lenge exists to improve things.

If you are fearful, you see difficultie in every opportunity. If you are fear-free, you see opportunities in every difficul .

Fear protects what I have from being taken away. But it also disconnects me from the rest of the world. In other words, fear keeps me separate and alone.

Here's the exciting part of Golas's message: With this new understanding of contraction and expansion, we can become completely attuned to where we are at all times.

If I am afraid, suspicious, skeptical, and resistant, I am in a contracted state. If I am joyful, open, interested, and willing, I am in an expanded state. Just knowing this puts me on an expanded path. Always remembering this, Golas says, brings enlightenment, which opens me even more.

Such openness gives me the ability to freely access my options. And taking advantage of options is the best part of change. Just as there are infinite ways to greet a customer, there are infinite ways to run your business. If you believe Thaddeus Golas, your most exciting option is to be open to all of them.

Because your life is lived on a continuum between the most contracted and most expanded - the most closed and most open - states, change is best understood as the movement from one to the other, and back again.

Most of the small business owners I've met see change as a thing-in-itself, as something that just happens to them. Most experience change as a threat. Whenever change shows up at the door, they quickly slam it. Many bolt the door and pile up the furniture. Some even run for their guns.

Few of them understand that change isn't a thing-in-itself, but rather the manifestation of many things. You might call it the revelation of all possibilities. Think of it as the ability at any moment to sacrifice what we are for what we could become.

Change can either challenge us or threaten us. It's our choice. Our attitude toward change can either pave the way to success or throw up a roadblock.

Change is where opportunity lives. Without change we would stay exactly as we are. The universe would be frozen still. Time would end.

At any given moment, we are somewhere on the path between a contracted and expanded state. Most of us are in the middle of the journey, neither totally closed nor totally open. According to Golas, change is our movement from one place in the middle toward one of the two ends.

Do you want to move toward contraction or toward enlightenment? Because without change, you are hopelessly stuck with what you've got.

Without change,

- we have no hope;
- we cannot know true joy;

- we will not get better; and
- we will continue to focus exclusively on what we have and the threat of losing it.

All of this negativity contracts us even more, until, at the extreme closed end of the spectrum, we become a black hole so dense that no light can escape.

Sadly, the harder we try to hold on to what we've got, the less able we are to do so. So we try still harder, which eventually drags us even deeper into the black hole of contraction.

Are you like that? Do you know anybody who is?

Think of change as the movement between where we are and where we're not. That leaves only two directions for change: either moving forward or slipping backward. We either become more contracted or more expanded.

The next step is to link change to how we feel. If we feel afraid, change is dragging us backward. If we feel open, change is pushing us forward.

Change is not a thing in itself, but a movement of our consciousness. By tuning in, by paying attention, we get clues to the state of our being.

Change, then, is not an outcome or something to be acquired. Change is a shift of our consciousness, of our being, of our humanity, of our attention, of our relationship with all other beings in the universe.

We are either "more in relationship" or "less in relationship." Change is the movement in either of those directions. The exciting part is that *we possess the ability to decide which way we go ... and to know in the moment which way we're moving.*

Closed, open... Open, closed. Two directions in the universe. The choice is yours.

Do you see the profound opportunity available to you? What an extraordinary way to live!

Enlightenment is not reserved for the sainted. Rather, it comes to us as we become more sensitive to ourselves. Eventually, we become our own guides, alerting ourselves to our state, moment by moment: *open ... closed ... open ... closed.*

Listen to your inner voice, your ally, and feel what it's like to be open and closed. Experience the instant of choice in both directions.

You will feel the awareness growing. It may be only a flash at first, so be alert. This feeling is accessible, but only if you avoid the black hole of contraction.

Are you afraid that you're totally contracted? Don't be - it's doubtful. The fact that you're still reading this book suggests that you're moving in the opposite direction.

You're more like a running back seeking the open field. You can see the opportunity gleaming in the distance. In the *open* direction.

Understand that I'm not saying that change itself is a point on the path; rather, it's the all-important movement.

Change is *in you*, not *out there.*

What path are you on? The path of liberation? Or the path of crystallization?

As we know, change can be for the better or for the worse.

If change is happening *inside* of you, it is for the worse only if you remain closed to it. The key, then, is your attitude - your acceptance or rejection of change. Change can be for the better only if you accept it. And it will certainly be for the worse if you don't.

Remember, change is nothing in itself. Without you, change doesn't exist. Change is happening inside of each of us, giving us clues to where we are at any point in time.

Rejoice in change, for it's a sign you are alive.

Are we open? Are we closed? If we're open, good things are bound to happen. If we're closed, things will only get worse.

According to Golas, it's as simple as that. Whatever happens defines where we are. *How* we are is *where* we are. It cannot be any other way.

For change is life.

Charles Darwin wrote, "It is not the strongest of the species that survive, nor the most intelligent, but the one that proves itself most responsive to change."

The growth of your home cleaning business, then, is its openness to change. Your role is to go with it, to be with it, to share the joy, embrace the opportunities, meet the challenges, learn the lessons.

Remember, there are three kinds of people: (1) those who make things happen, (2) those who let things happen, and (3) those who wonder what the hell happened. The people who make things happen are masters of change. The other two are its victims.

Which type are you?

The Big Change

If all this is going to mean anything to the life of your company, you have to know when you're going to leave it. At what point, as your home cleaning business rises from where it is now to where it can ultimately grow, are you going to sell it? Because if you don't have a clear picture of when you want out, your business is the master of your destiny, not the reverse.

As we stated earlier, the most valuable form of money is equity, and unless your business vision includes your equity and how you will use it to your advantage, you will forever be consumed by your business.

Your business is potentially the best friend you ever had. It is your business's nature to serve you, so let it. If, however, you are not a wise steward, if you do not tell your business what you expect from it, it will run rampant, abuse you, use you, and confuse you.

Change. Growth. Equity.

Focus on the point in the future when you will take leave of your business. Now reconsider your goals in that context. Be specific. rite them down.

Skipping this step is like tiptoeing through earthquake country. Who can say where the fault line is waiting? And who knows exactly when your whole world may come crashing down around you?

Which brings us to the subject of *time*. But first, let's take in Russell's thoughts regarding *change*.

CHAPTER

20

Staying Ahead of Change

Russell O'Connell

"*Change before you have to.*"

—Jack Welch, former CEO of General Electric

As Michael wrote: life *is* change. From the cradle to the grave, we—and the world around us—inevitably change. The big question is whether we're going to embrace change, and win. Or resist it, and lose.

This is no fridge-magnet cliché. It's the hard truth. Change means new facts, and facts are facts. You can live by leveraging these facts, or—at your own peril—you can deny them and try to bend reality to fit your fantasy world. It s a binary choice.

In practice, however, this choice is often not very clear to us. We, as human beings, need to have a way of mentally organizing our realities. So, we have a strong tendency to label ourselves, others and things around us to find meaning—a framework for how this unfathomable world works. We construct stories of who we are and what we're supposed to do in life. Because of this, we'll always have a degree of what's referred to as observer bias—we tend to notice things that we think are relevant to our internal storytelling, and we tend to push our interpretation of what we see to fit this narrative

And, oftentimes, change is so slow, so relatively imperceptible, that it's easy enough to discount the difference between our own narrative and the actual reality. It's not like trying to fit a square peg through a round hole—it's more like pushing a somewhat oval peg through that hole. It doesn't quite fit, but it's close enough for us to make it work.

We end up believing what we want to believe.

Maybe you've heard of how you can place a frog in cold water and very slowly bring the water to a boil, killing the frog, which didn't notice what was going on because the change was so slow, so gradual. Now, that story is actually a myth. The frog *will* get out of the water well before it risks getting boiled. But the myth is still useful as an allegory:

Most home-cleaning business owners refuse to embrace change, telling themselves that they have "just enough." Just enough money. Just enough time. Just enough moments with the family. Just enough rest. They're busy doing, and they keep congratulating themselves on being "successful", when all they're really doing is carrying out tactical tasks. Like the frog in the myth, they're lulling themselves into feeling that everything is fine

And then it's suddenly all over.

Chances are that, right now, you're somewhere on that path. You built your home-cleaning company to create *a job* for you. Almost as an afterthought, since you've had some success, you're being tempted to believe "*maybe this could actually work out as a proper business!*"

At this point, you find yourself at a critical crossroads

Your decision here will marginally impact your business in the short term, but dramatically impact it in terms of the value and equity you can get from it in 5-10 years. The choice is essentially between remaining the "doer" that you've probably prided yourself on being or becoming a *creator*. There's a vast difference between the two

As a doer, you're busy just doing things—or, put another way, *reacting* to things that "happen to you." You're busy working *in* your business.

This is the easy choice for many, because it doesn't require much by way of change, something that people are so resistant to. You can go on *doing* things in a similar fashion for decades. Just don't expect a different outcome. Your business in twenty years, if it still somehow exists after the tremendous changes that society will have undergone by then, will look much the same as it does today. You and your staff will be busy *doing*, reacting to what the world throws at you and making "enough" to feel "successful". Everything will be "fine"

Frog-style.

By contrast, as a creator, you work *on* your business, actively *instigating change*—you are proactive, staying ahead of the changes that will inevitably come.

Like Jack Welch said, "change before you have to."

Of course, there will be changes that you couldn't see coming. Things like the global financial crisis in 2008 (or as we like to call it down here, the "GFC"), Covid or a sudden change in taxation laws which can encourage or discourage private customers from using household services. And sometimes, such black swan events actually force you to improve your business.

For instance, during the Covid-pandemic, Melbourne was locked down tighter than most other places in the world outside of China. As a result, many restaurants ended up closing for good. But many also chose to create highly efficien online ordering and delivery services, and they didn't only make it through the pandemic—their new systems were so efficient they kept them even after the lockdowns ended. The outside change forced a positive transformation of their businesses.

The good news is that with a system in place, you can model various scenarios to see what your business could withstand, should this or that unexpected event occur. Check what would be the flow-on effects if you suddenly had five staff members quit, if you lost a dozen customers in a month, or if all the cars in your fleet were recalled due to a manufacturing fault. You can come up with just about anything and see how the system could handle it.

Without a system, you obviously can't do that. It then becomes a matter of drawing up distinct plans for all these events (in effect, creating different systems to deal with each situation), and that's simply not tenable.

So, a strong system makes your business more resilient. But, as per previous chapters, it's also inherently engineered to facilitate growth. With the right system, your profits *will* grow—and this is also a type of change that you must be mentally prepared for.

Selling and exiting your business is the biggest change of all, and it's imperative that you plan for it. Set a date for when you want to have built your business to a certain level, after which selling and exiting will at least be an ever-present option. This virtually forces you to start approaching your business with a systems-based mindset. Because without a plan, without a system, you'll quickly find that there's no way to calculate your growth and exit date.

You know why most people don't do this? Because it's difficul and daunting. It's much, much easier to just keep doing what you already know how to do and congratulate yourself on a job well done: "today I cleaned five homes, good on me!" But you're always paid for the role you play in life—and guess who gets paid the most, the technician/doer taking the job or the entrepreneur/creator who defined it

Without fail, it's the entrepreneur/creator.

The repetitive tasks of the doer means that a lot of people could fill that role, and the pay will be set accordingly. Which means that *working* your way to wealth takes a long time, if you ever arrive there. By contrast, creative ideas can be invaluable. It's perfectly feasible to sell the IP rights to a concept for millions of dollars if it's strong enough.

You can *think* your way to wealth in a very short time frame.

We see this happening all the time—in the news, on social media, in the periodicals of our industry. Big companies buying small companies that are doing things differentl .

Google buying a startup for multiple millions of dollars because they see how the system the new company has created can be applied within Google.

Amazon buying a tiny tech company with an app no one uses for eight figures because it's going to fundamentally change the state of Amazon's business worldwide.

A restaurant group buying a digital marketing company for the training systems they've created and used.

Bear all this in mind as you're standing at this crossroads. Choose to see your business as a strategic concept to develop and sell rather than a tactical job to do (and do and do and do…).

Play your cards right, and you could have qualified buyers lining up in only a few years' time—savvy entrepreneurs who are impressed with the proven, scalable system you've built and will pay handsomely for it. They are buying a turnkey system with the aim of developing it further and selling it for even more money.

Treat your business as a job, however, and you could easily find yourself working hard for decades before you sell to another technician, who will essentially only be paying for your client list. That technician is just buying themselves a job with the (aimless) aim of keeping on working in that job.

Bottom line: no matter which path you take, you will be working hard for the next few years, so why not make sure that you'll eventually have something to show for it other than callused hands!?

Looking back into the future

What, then, are the changes that you should prepare for? What does the future hold? Who knows, really!? But, whilst history might not necessarily repeat itself, it can sure pay to take a look in the rear-view mirror.

Assuming that you're over 30 years old, you have seen the world change fundamentally. Things we take for granted today were mere fantasies (if that!) when you were born. Who would have imagined this future, where our cars talk to us, where artificial intelligence creates images, video, sound and text, where you can simply jump online to see satellite pictures of every last corner of Earth?

This development has occurred at blistering speed. Your smartphone, for example, already has a computing power hundreds of times more powerful than that of the space program that put astronauts on the moon. And the pace is only picking up. With AI teaching itself to become increasingly potent and accurate, the foreseeable future—even just the next few years—are bound to bring further disruptive changes.

One thing is as sure as sure can be. The future will be increasingly governed by increasingly powerful AI based digital systems.

This is actually great news for you as the owner of a home-cleaning business. Because there are many industries where humans will be wholly or partially replaced by AI, both in blue- and white-collar business. Accountants and lawyers and stock traders will at the very least have to learn to master AI, but chances are that they, too, eventually will be made redundant in their current roles. Indeed, you will be hard pressed to find industries where AI won't have any impact at all

Artificial intelligence, however, cannot wipe down a tabletop or clean your fridge, and whilst there are vacuum robots and the like, personal cleaning services will most likely remain superior to automated options for a long time yet.

This is why you, the savvy entrepreneur, should be able to see the fantastic business opportunity in the home-cleaning sector. On the one hand, most of your competitors have no system or standards in place—and they have delicate or non-existent personal relationships to their customers.

On the other hand, you have amazing technology right at your fingertips—technology that you could use to create strong systems, exact standards and close relationships to a premium customer base. Digital systems engineered to embrace change and organically produce one key outcome: ever-increasing growth in profits

Really, with all of the above in mind, ask yourself this: am I really in the cleaning industry? Am I really someone who cleans other people's homes?

No—that's something you can leave for your competitors.

You are *the creator and owner of a digital business that sells time to people whose time is a worth a lot.*

This is our strategy at MyHome. Creative thinking expressed through highly efficien technology, such as our proprietary app MyOP™, which handles everything from scheduling, invoicing and payroll, to hiring, marketing and data analysis.

Standards.

Systems.

Digital tools.

Logical, finely calibrated pieces of engineering. But what really drives me and the MyHome staff is something highly emotional. A deep appreciation—a reverence—for life itself. We know that there is no commodity more precious than what we're selling. Time. At the end of the day, it's all that we human beings have—and we only get so much of it.

If you truly take ownership of this fact, you WILL start changing things in your life. Like someone who has survived a major health scare, you will value each and every moment. And when you do that in your business, you'll find there's no better way to make the most of your time, of your life, than to employ systems-based thinking.

Value life—and you will intuitively systemise your business.

That's why the next couple of chapters will be about just this.

The time of *your* life.

CHAPTER

21

On the Subject of Time

Michael E. Gerber

"Money and time are the heaviest burdens of life and ... the unhappiest of all mortals are those who have more of either than they know how to use."

—Samuel Johnson

"I'm running out of time!" small business owners often lament. "I've got to learn how to manage my time more carefully!"

Of course, they see no real solution to this problem. They're just worrying the subject to death. Singing the blues of the small business owner, especially those involved in the home cleaning industry.

Some make a real effort to control time. Maybe they go to time management classes, or faithfully try to record their activities during every hour of the day.

But it's hopeless. Even when these technicians work harder, even when they keep precise records of their time, there's always a shortage of it. It's as if they're looking at a square clock in a round universe. Something doesn't fit. The result: their home cleaning business is constantly chasing time, and as the owner, they're constantly chasing work, money, and life.

And the reason is simple. The technicians who own home cleaning businesses don't see time for what it really is. They think of time with a small "t," rather than Time with a capital "T."

Yet, Time is simply another word for *your life*. It's your ultimate asset, your gift at birth - and you can spend it any way you want. Do you know how you want to spend it? Do you have a plan?

How do *you* deal with Time? Are you even conscious of it? If you are, I bet you are constantly locked into either the future or the past. Relying on either memory or imagination.

Do you recognize these voices? "Once I get through this, I can have a drink ... go on a vacation ... retire." "I remember when I first started out and cleaning homes was satisfying.

As you go to bed at midnight, are you thinking about waking up at 5:00 a.m. so that you can try to do some administrative work in the offic before you get to the first house at 7:30 a.m., *and* you've got a full schedule *and* a new customer scheduled for 2:30?

Most of us are prisoners of the future or the past. While pinballing between the two, we miss the richest moments of our life - the present. Trapped forever in memory or imagination, we are strangers to the here and now. Our future is nothing more than an extension of our past, and the present is merely the background.

It's sobering to think that right now each of us is at a precise spot somewhere between the beginning of our Time (our birth) and the end of our Time (our death).

No wonder everyone frets about Time. What really terrifies us is that *we're using up our life and we can't stop it.*

It feels as if we're plummeting toward the end with nothing to break our free fall. Time is out of control! Understandably, this is horrifying, mostly because the real issue is not time with a small "t" but Death with a big "D."

From the depths of our existential anxiety, we try to put Time in a different perspective - all the while pretending we can manage it. We talk about Time as though it were something other than what it is. "Time is money," we announce, as though that explains it.

But what every business owner in the home cleaning industry *should* know is that Time is life. And Time ends! Life ends!

The big, walloping, irresolvable problem is that *we don't know how much Time we have left!*

Do you feel the fear? Do you want to get over it?

Let's look at Time more seriously.

To fully grasp Time with a capital "T," you have to ask the Big Question: *How do I wish to spend the rest of my Time?*

Because I can assure you that if you don't ask that Big Question with a big "Q," you will forever be assailed by the little questions. You'll shrink the whole of your life to *this time* and *next time* and the *last time* - all the while wondering, *what time is it?*

It's like running around the deck of a sinking ship worrying about where you left the keys to your cabin.

You must accept that you have only so much Time; that you're using up that Time second by precious second. And that your Time, your life, is the most valuable asset you have. Of course, you can use your Time any way you want. But unless you choose to use it as richly, as rewardingly, as excitingly, as intelligently, as *intentionally* as possible, you'll squander it and fail to appreciate it.

Indeed, if you are oblivious to the value of your Time, you'll commit the single greatest sin: You will live your life unconscious of its passing you by.

Until you deal with Time with a capital "T," you'll worry about time with a small "t" until you have no Time—or life—left. Then your Time will be history … along with your life.

I can anticipate the question: If Time is the problem, why not just take on fewer customers? Well, that's certainly an option, but probably not necessary. I know of several home cleaning businesses (including Russell's) that see many times more customers than the average, yet they don't work long hours. How is it possible?

These entrepreneurs have a system. The majority of what needs to be done or communicated to customers is "downloaded" to the field teams and offic staff. By using this expert system, the employees can do everything the owner would do—everything that isn't owner-dependent.

Be Versus Do

Remember when we all asked, "What do I want to be when I grow up?" It was one of our biggest concerns as children.

Notice that the question isn't, "What do I want to *do* when I grow up?" It's "What do I want to *be*?"

Shakespeare wrote, "To be or not to be." Not "To do or not to do."

But when you grow up, people always ask you, "What do you *do?*" How did the question change from *being* to *doing*? How did we miss the critical distinction between the two?

Even as children, we sensed the distinction. The real question we were asking was not what we would end up *doing* when we grew up, but who we would *be*.

We were talking about a *life* choice, not a *work* choice. We instinctively saw it as a matter of how we spend our Time, not what we do *in* time.

Look to children for guidance. I believe that as children we instinctively saw Time as life and tried to use it wisely. As children, we wanted to make a life choice, not a work choice. As children, we didn't know - or care - that work had to be done on time, on budget.

Until you see Time for what it really is - your life span - you will always ask the wrong question.

Until you embrace the whole of your Time and shape it accordingly, you will never be able to fully appreciate the moment.

Until you fully appreciate every second that comprises Time, you will never be sufficientl motivated to live those seconds fully.

Until you're sufficientl motivated to live those seconds fully, you will never see fit to change the way you are. You will never take the quality and sanctity of Time seriously.

And unless you take the sanctity of Time seriously, you will continue to struggle to catch up with something behind you. Your frustrations will mount as you try to snatch the second that just whisked by.

If you constantly fret about time with a small "t," then big-"T" Time will blow right past you. And you'll miss the whole point, the real truth about Time: You can't manage it; you never could. You can only *live* it.

And so that leaves you with these questions: How do I live my life? How do I give significance to it? How can I be here now, in this moment?

Once you begin to ask these questions, you'll find yourself moving toward a much fuller, richer life. But if you continue to be caught up in the banal work you do every day, you're never going to find the time to take a deep breath, exhale, and be present in the now.

So, let's talk about the subject of *work*. But first, let's read what Russell has done with his *time*.

CHAPTER

22

The Time of Your Life

Russell O'Connell

"Lack of direction, not lack of time, is the problem. We all have twenty-four-hour days."

-Zig Ziglar

It's interesting to read Michael's ideas on Time, isn't it?

You're likely thinking, "*Sure, Russell, but "time" to me isn't that deep. I'm kind of stuck wrestling this monster of a business I created, and there are precious few days I can afford to think so philosophically about time.*"

That's kind of the point of this chapter; indeed, this whole book.

At MyHome, our slogan is, "We do clean … you do life™".

Those words aren't solely applied to our clients. They also apply to our people, from the top down.

MyHome was designed to give time back to *every* life we touch, from our customers to our teams, franchise partners, and leaders—to everyone involved in our business.

Think about it: the challenges all of us are facing when we discuss "Time" are really indicative of how you're running your home-cleaning business (and your life), aren't they?

The real problem isn't so much "time" in terms of hours, minutes, and seconds, it's the value you place on them and the choices you make—and those habits begin to form the minute you decide to open your home-cleaning business.

It's worth noting that both Michael and I have already pointed out that many new or small home-cleaning companies are owned by men and women who don't place a value on their time—and as those companies grow, those bad habits create challenges.

You must move beyond those poor habits.

Right now, you have a decision to make, and it literally is the *only* next step. Refuse to do it and you might as well put this book down and go back to the grind, because it's that important.

Place a dollar value on your time. What's your time really worth? Think about it. Really think about it.

Because until you demand more of yourself as a business owner *and person*, and you begin to live with that value in mind every hour of every day, you're flatly refusing to *live*.

No matter what dollar value you initially put on your time, here's a good rule of thumb: if you find yourself being busy doing simple, low-value repetitive tasks, that's an indication that you're not using your time wisely. Being busy "doing" is for the technicians. To the greatest extent possible, you should be busy *creating*—thinking strategically and refining your systems to ensure that every minute you put in now will make future minutes more profitable

Again, you shouldn't be busy working *in* your business. You should be busy working *on* your business.

Here's another really important point in this. When it comes to creativity, time is highly relative. Just ask yourself, how long did it take for you to come up with a brilliant idea? It presented itself in the blink of an eye, didn't it!? Sure, in some cases, there's a lot of research and analysis to be done before you know WHAT it is that you want to create, but how long does it take for the ideas themselves to form once they do arrive? Virtually no time at all, right!?

In other words: it's perfectly possible for you to sit down with a focus on developing new ideas for how your staff manage day-to-day chores—and revolutionise your entire business and create immense value in a single afternoon.

Furthermore, when you put a value on your own time, you adopt the mindset of your customer base. They put a high value on their own time too, and they will appreciate and respect that you put a similarly high value on yours.

Remember, in practice, you won't be the owner of a "home-cleaning" company as much as the entrepreneur behind a digital business that sells time to people whose time is worth a lot. Present yourself accordingly, and you'll find it a whole lot easier to establish rapport and create trusting relationships with a likeminded clientele.

Now, business conversations about time often turn into a discussion about efficien . After all, people are so used to media and marketing telling them that they just need to "work faster" to make more money, right?

That's missing the point by a wide margin.

As per the above, you should not work *in* your business, being busy *doing* things in a more or less efficien way. That's for your staff. You will not *work* yourself to wealth as a technician anyway.

You will *create* wealth by putting a value on your time and working *on* your business.

When I start talking about time, this is my message: make your time as valuable as possible and sell time to those who put the highest value on theirs.

That can only be achieved if you create systems and populate them with staff who take care of the tactical work for you, leaving you free to do the high-value, strategic work of the entrepreneur.

If you're still in a place in your home-cleaning business where you're doing the work of the Technician, then at least mitigate and manage that time.

Perhaps you're like a friend of mine in the United States, who simply MUST have all the tactical work of his company sorted Monday-Tuesday-Wednesday. Only then does he feel that he can focus efficientl on his administrative and leadership responsibilities, which he covers on Wednesday evenings. He reserves all day Thursday and half his Friday for entrepreneurial work. And come Friday afternoon? He closes his computer, directs his work phone to an answering service, and considers his time with his family to be sacrosanct.

He turns his phone on at 7:10 a.m. on Monday morning, when his son gets on the bus to school.

You can do the same while you're learning and leveling up as an Entrepreneur. For example, you could streamline your cleaning appointments into three days each week, allowing you time to work *on* your business.

Also, you don't have to do all of this strategic work alone. Ask your team for input. For instance, they could document how they carry out certain tasks that you're not competent at.

Explain the way you want it documented, of course, but use their expertise, too!

"Alice, this week, I'd like you to do me a favor, please? As you're going through the homes you're cleaning, please note which rooms you start in, and roughly how long those take to clean to our standard. Could you also write down the travel route you take between clients' homes and how much travel time you deal with each day?"

You'd have a simple form Alice could easily fill out. Then you can document her systems and see what insights and metrics they give you. Of course, Alice might be asking 20 questions about this, and your answers aren't about the "why" of this, only about her steps. Give this same assignment to all your people, and some will have fifteen pages of notes on their own processes, while others struggle to have two.

But that's *everything*: how your team handles new clients, how your team restocks supplies, how you meet prospective customers, the process for quoting.

For billing.

For scheduling.

Even for dealing with something as mundane as traffi or road construction.

Or something as important as bringing a new client's home up to a replicable level of cleanliness right from the first visit

You'll continually analyze these pieces and steps and adjust them. You'll scrap some, adjust others, and realize that this or that one simply doesn't produce the results you want. Each one has its place in your Operations Manual.

Yes, this takes time to create, and time to document, and time to refine. Time that you don't think you have

Guess what?

Not doing it takes time, too!

Every day, you've got 86,400 seconds, the vast majority of which lie unclaimed and underutilized at the end of the day.

There's a reason I've asked you to think about this, and it's deceptively simple: *until you begin to value every moment, you'll simply waste them.*

With clients.

With employees.

With your spouse.

With your children.

With *yourself.*

I can tell you this as a man who has built a successful business based on cleaning homes: the real work of entrepreneurship in our industry isn't about making money, it's about making *time.*

It's what you choose to do with your seconds, minutes and hours that will decide as to whether you can exit your home-cleaning business with millions of dollars in your pocket within the next few years.

The decisions you make—or don't make—about how you'll conduct and operate your business will also impact on the satisfaction you take from it, day to day, week to week, over the entire course of your ownership.

Within your business, you can—and should—aspire to hand off tasks that you really don't care for. Take that administrative work, for example. I've met few people who are fans of that. And it's absolutely fine to recognize you hate certain tasks—I certainly know what I will and won't do within the confines of MyHome. You simply do three things: recognize what systems are needed, create them, and hire those tasks out!

I've already mentioned I have little desire to actually clean a home (although I could, because I'd simply follow the Tricolour™ system). Ditto my feelings about most administrative work. On the other hand, I love the hiring and training processes, so much of my time is now spent in that area. The end result, for me, is that *I enjoy the work I do each day.*

Why not make your journey enjoyable, too? There will always be challenges no matter what route you choose, but there's NO reason you should believe the rest of your life is going to be grueling and mind-numbing work that will leave you broke and broken.

Spend your time—every second of it—wisely.

CHAPTER

23

On the Subject of Work

Michael E. Gerber

"They intoxicate themselves with work so they don't see how they really are."

—Aldous Huxley

In the business world, as the saying goes, the entrepreneur knows something about everything, the technician knows everything about something, and the switchboard operator just knows everything.

In a home-cleaning business, owners often see their natural work as the work of the technician. The Supreme Technician. Often to the exclusion of everything else.

After all, most of these owners had zero preparation working as a manager and spent no time thinking as an entrepreneur—those aren't courses commonly taught in colleges or even mentioned in the periodicals of the home-cleaning industry. By the time they own their own home-cleaning business, they're just doing it, doing it, doing it.

At the same time, they want everything---freedom, respect, money. Most of all, they want to rid themselves of meddling bosses and start their own business. That way they can be their own boss and take home all the money. These technicians are in the throes of an entrepreneurial seizure.

Men and women who have been praised for their amazing skills elsewhere believe they have what it takes to run a home-cleaning business. It's not unlike the plumber who becomes a contractor because he's a great plumber. Sure, he may be a great plumber … but it doesn't necessarily follow that he knows how to build a plumbing business to do this work.

It's the same for your home-cleaning company! So many of these owners are surprised to wake up one morning and discover that they're nowhere near as equipped for owning their own business as they thought they were.

More than any other subject, work is the cause of obsessive-compulsive behavior by small business owners.

Work. You've got to do it every single day.

Work. If you fall behind, you'll pay for it.

Work. There's either too much or not enough.

So many home cleaners describe work as what they do when they're busy. Some discriminate between the work they *could* be doing as owners and the work they *should* be doing as owners.

But according to The E-Myth, those are exactly the same thing. The work you *could* do and the work you *should* do as the owner of a home cleaning business is identical. Let me explain.

Strategic Work versus Tactical Work

In your business, you can do only two kinds of work: strategic work and tactical work.

Tactical work is easier to understand, because it's what almost every home cleaner does almost every minute of every hour of every day. It's called getting the job done. It's called doing business.

Tactical work includes cleaning, vacuuming, sweeping, dusting, customer education, managing subcontractors, marketing, filing, billing, bookkeeping, writing emails, quoting jobs, returning calls, going to the bank, and seeing customers.

The E-Myth says that tactical work is all the work owners find themselves doing in a home cleaning business to *avoid* doing the strategic work.

"I'm too busy," most of these owners will tell you.

"How come nothing goes right unless I do it myself?" they complain in frustration.

These owners say these things when they're up to their ears in tactical work. But most of these Technicians don't understand that if they had done more strategic work, they would have less tactical work to do.

On the other hand, in your home cleaning business, you're doing strategic work when you choose ask the following questions:

- Why am I in the home cleaning industry?
- What will my business look like when it's done?
- What must my business look, act, and feel like in order for it to compete successfully?
- What are the key indicators of my business?

Please note that I said entrepreneurs *ask* these questions when they are doing strategic work. I didn't say these are the questions they necessarily answer.

That is the fundamental difference between strategic work and tactical work. Tactical work is all about *answers*: How to do this. How to do that.

Strategic work, in contrast, is all about *questions:* What business are we really in? Why are we in that business? Who specifically is our business determined to serve? When will I sell this business? How and where will this business be doing business when I sell it? And so forth.

Not that strategic questions don't have answers. Entrepreneurs who commonly ask strategic questions know that once they ask such a question, they're already on their way to *envisioning* the answer. Question and answer are part of a whole. You can't find the right answer until you've asked the right question.

Tactical work is much easier, because the question is always more obvious. In fact, you don't ask the tactical question; instead, the question arises from a result you need to get or from a problem you need to solve. Billing a customer is tactical work. Cleaning a home is tactical work. Firing an employee is tactical work. Cleaning a kitchen is tactical work.

Tactical work is the stuff you do every day in your business. Strategic work is the stuff you plan to do to create an exceptional sole proprietorship / business / enterprise.

In tactical work, the question comes from *out there* rather than *in here*. The tactical question is about something *outside* of you, whereas the strategic question is about something *inside* of you.

The tactical question is about something you *need* to do, whereas the strategic question is about something you *want* to do. Want versus need.

If tactical work consumes you,

- you are always reacting to something outside of you;
- your business runs you; you don't run it;
- your employees run you; you don't run them; and
- your life runs you; you don't run your life.

You must understand that the more strategic work you do, the more intentional your decisions, your business, and your life become. *Intention* is the byword of strategic work.

Everything on the outside begins to serve you, to serve your vision, rather than forcing you to serve it. Everything you *need* to do is congruent with what you *want* to do. It means you have a vision, an aim, a purpose, a strategy, an *envisioned* result.

Strategic work is the work you do to *design* your business, to design your life.

Tactical work is the work you do to *implement* the design created by strategic work.

Without strategic work, there is no design. Without strategic work, all that's left is keeping busy.

There's only one thing left to do. It's time to take *action.*

But first, let s read what Russell has to say about *work.*

CHAPTER

24

Working ON Your Business

Russell O'Connell

"How can I systematize my business in such a way that it could be replicated 5,000 times, so the 5,000th unit would run as smoothly as the first? How can I own my business, and still be free of it? How can I spend my time doing the work I love to do rather than the work I have to do?"

Michael E. Gerber, The E-Myth Revisited: *Why Most Small Businesses Don't Work and What to Do About It*

Not all of life is work. But work is all life.

A popular catch phrase these days is "work-life balance"—as if life starts *after* work.

I've always found it funny that so many people spend their workweeks pining for the weekend. As if there should be something stopping them from thoroughly enjoying their time at work—as though work doesn't really count as part of your available lifetime. But this makes no sense. You spend the vast majority of all daytime hours of all your prime years in life at work.

If you're not enjoying work—if you're not actively looking forward to going to work—you're missing out on life. Simple as that.

Don't get me wrong. I'm not a workaholic, and I treasure my time with family and friends above all else. But even when you've reached a point of financial independence, you need something to challenge you, to inspire you, to make you feel that you're making a difference in the world. And for me, that's improving my business, thereby enriching other people's lives.

These inspirational challenges, as you mature from a technician to an entrepreneur, I assure you, will not include vacuuming and wiping down tabletops. The work you'll be doing on your business is highly intellectual, strategic, and creative.

Creativity, by definition, has no limits and is all about developing *new* things. Ask yourself questions like what new systems you could implement to provide better service to your customers?

How could you use technology to cut down time spent on tedious tasks like accounting and administration?

What will tomorrow's technology mean to your business?

How can you make work more enjoyable for your employees?

What training could you implement to make them take ownership of what they're doing?

All such questions are profoundly meaningful, and as long as your creative thinking has got a worthwhile goal, you'll never ever get bored with it. What's more, knowing that the resulting systems will make you go from strength to strength is all the carrot you need. You can put the stick away.

Speaking of being too hard on yourself, know this: you cannot work strategically and creatively all day every day. Well, sure, you can be present at the offic and *attempt* to crack new ideas during all work hours. But don't expect yourself to be productive all that time. Chances are, rather, that you'll grow frustrated and start blaming yourself for not being creative enough, and that will put a damper on your inspiration and creativity really quick.

There's a reason you find ping-pong tables, gaming machines and indoor relaxation gardens at advertising agencies. It's not that professional strategists and creatives are slack. It's that they know that being in the right frame of mind when working is invaluable.

As per my previous chapter, you can come up with brilliant ideas in next to no time—if you are mentally prepared for it. So, find the ways that work for you. My personal tip: get up early! Make yourself a tea or coffee, go through your emails and get your day started hours before anyone else even gets out of bed. You'll have some really good, quiet quality time—and, if you're anything like me, you'll probably find that the great ideas simply come to you then.

Another tip: set yourself the goal of working on only three strategic things every day. You decide just how much progress you're going to make on each.

And once you get there, stop. You're done for the day!

Rationale: if you set about trying to build and create system after system, you'll simply be exchanging the "busy-ness" of the Technician with the "busy-ness" of the Entrepreneur.

Like an alcoholic who has sworn off the bottle and still yearns for a pint now and then, this need to constantly be "doing something" will lead you to channel your energies *somewhere*. When I speak to people in the industry, a recurring theme for many is how they're approaching strategic work with a tactical mindset.

In some cases, they've made a list of "everything" they need company-wide, and they jump wholeheartedly into that list, "Busy! Busy! Busy!, Doin' it, doin' it, doin' it!" and when they can't see immediate improvements, they assume Michael's ideas don't work.

Nonsense!

The ideas DO work, but you have to orient yourself in such a way as to observe the improvements.

In my experience when it comes to strategic work, concentrate on only three things per day. That's it.

Perhaps that's creating or refining training programs; perhaps that's your technology stack; perhaps it's the workflow of your content creation. Whatever it is, manage your expectations and watch how far you extend yourself. Because when you attempt to juggle and create too much, you simply can't do it.

This is in stark contrast to what those "influencers" and "gurus" and "time management hacks" we all hear about imply, but—and stay with me here—if you approach the very real problem of how to accomplish strategic work as a technician, you'll create a huge list and never get it done.

As an example, our Technician sits down on a Sunday morning because he's ready to "create" a real home-cleaning company. He begins to think through what's needed in his business. As the morning passes, he fills up page after page with what his company will be, and as noon approaches, he leans back in his chair and beholds what he's outlined.

Page after page of *more* work to be done—and he's already working 50 hours a week IN his company!

The truth is, any entrepreneurial desire likely burns out right there.

"*It's too much to ever do!*"

"*My business isn't perfect, but it's good enough.*"

"*Gerber is full of it!*"

Now, let me tell you how I've approached this same process… and been wildly successful.

I *did* sit down and think about what was needed. I *did* envision the end result of a well-built company, and I *did* have a seemingly endless list of things to accomplish—and that list grew every day. But instead of being overwhelmed, I chose the three things I could concentrate on, create and build that would have the most immediate impact on MyHome's success.

I built them out, studied the impact, and then—*with the impact known*—I reviewed my list and identified the *next* three things.

Thus, I could sort three items, see the tangible result of the work I was doing, and not fall victim to overwhelm. At the same time, I had the sense of satisfaction we all get from making progress. These small but tangible, incremental steps forward are the keys to our collective success as entrepreneurs.

Identify-Create-Observe

Taking this approach in nice, easy steps, will enable you to evolve from a harried Technician or an overwhelmed Manager into an enlightened Entrepreneur.

If you, step by step, make progress on three strategic solutions every week, that's potentially over 150 solutions you've built in a single year. Wow!

Thinking back to our unstated goal of having a viable business that can be sold in 3-10 years, imagine how robust an Operations Manual you can create if you have taken this time, diligently, week after week and year after year, to document hundreds of solutions. At a seemingly leisurely pace, you will have created a strategic system—a little money machine. You know exactly how this machine works, and you know exactly how to explain it to savvy prospect buyers, who will be ready to pay very, very handsomely for a proven, scalable business system.

What's more, you've had a lot of fun doing all of this!

What's Holding You Back?

In many ways, it's my belief that the biggest reason for MyHome's success isn't me. It's not Michael's intense focus on systems, or even just some lucky alignment of stars and planets.

It's my *lack of experience* in cleaning.

I'm certainly not an expert at it, I can think of no special insight I might have on how to do it "better" and I freely accept there are literally *billions* of people on this planet who can do it far better than I ever could.

Since I didn't know what could and couldn't be done in the home cleaning industry, I could truly approach the business from a strategic point of view, as the Entrepreneur, not the Technician.

Make no mistake, when you begin to do the *true* work of the Entrepreneur, you'll have to learn new things, you'll have to spend time in uncomfortable scenarios and create effective solutions to prevent their recurrence, and you'll inevitably have to learn to handle rejection, failure and growth.

Is that really any different than any other thing you've already faced in your life?

You weren't born knowing how to do anything—you've *learned* it. It's our nature to grow, so why wouldn't you approach your home-cleaning business with this same attitude and vigor?

Begin the true work of entrepreneurship today. Embrace the idea that you are to work ON your home-cleaning business, not merely IN it. It's perfectly fine that you don't know how to do this as yet—you're not supposed to!

But going into unknown territory is scary. It's so much more comfortable and convenient to keep doing what you already know how to do. This is one of the *actual* reasons why so many owners in the home-cleaning industry keep cleaning homes themselves. Another is this idea: it's so "easy" to do, why should you pay someone else to do it!?

That's exactly why you SHOULD pay someone else to do it. If it's easy, repetitive work, you should have created systems for exactly how it should be done and hire technicians to carry it out whilst you, the entrepreneur, work ON your business.

At this point in the discussion, I often hear business owners protesting that "nobody wants to work anymore" or "it's impossible to find good staff". That's simply not true. Trust me, people *do* want to work, but they've become selective when it comes to who and what they want to work *for*. Which brings us to the next point.

Creating a strong work culture

So far in this chapter, we've spoken about you, the entrepreneur, and your business systems. But what about the people who populate your systems? Your employees. You should treat them in a similar manner to how you treat yourself.

Make sure they can feel good about themselves at work. Maybe you think that's a given. But it's not.

Just think of an offic worker with an overflowing inbox. At some point, the company will simply quit giving them "more" work, because it's obvious they can't do anymore. But what of the workers who are steadily working through their inboxes?

The company continues to pile on more work.

How can that situation possibly be successful? How can the great worker ever feel great about themselves when the work is never-ending?

Now imagine a scenario where the workers begin each day—or week—with a specific number of tasks to be done, and when they're done, they simply go home?

There will certainly be more work tomorrow. But as for today? They're done. "Enjoy the rest of your day, Susan. See you in the morning!"

How inspiring would that job be?

How excited would Susan be?

But how will Susan know that she's done a great job? By your having set exact standards for all her tasks and enabled her to see when she's reached every goal for the day.

Also, make sure that everyone feels part of the team. When everyone knows what role they're playing, and how their collective efforts are paying off for the business as a whole, you can create a truly vibrant atmosphere.

At MyHome, we put the turnover, along with our other KPIs, on a digital whiteboard for everyone to see. There are no secrets. Everyone knows when a new franchise partner joins us, and we ring a bell every time we sign up a new customer. We enjoy each other's little wins, and we set incremental goals for ourselves, tracking our progress. Work becomes like a sport or a game. It takes focus and effort, sure, but it's also social, fun and inspiring—and this isn't lost on our prospect franchise partners and customers.

As my old friend Roy Grundy once told me, "Don't work from perspiration or desperation—work from inspiration".

Let's look at that word, "inspiration". What does it really *mean*?

Inspiration is derived from the Latin word *inspiratus*, which means to breathe in (and this is still the meaning in medical science—you might have heard doctors talking about inspiration in terms of lung capacity). But the literal meaning is actually predated by the figurative, which is "to breathe [divine influence] into"

In other words, the inspiration, what you breathe in, has a substance. What is that substance? To quote another great, the painter Henri Matisse, "Don't wait for inspiration. It comes while one is working." Inspiration, thus, is found in the substance of work itself.

Get immersed in your strategic thinking, your creativity and your new-born business systems. Breathe in all these concepts, and the inspiration for new great ideas will come to you. And what happens then?

You *take action*, and here's Michael telling you how…

CHAPTER

25

On the Subject of Taking Action

Michael E. Gerber

"You should know now that a man of knowledge lives by acting, not by thinking about acting, nor by thinking about what he will think when he has finished acting. A man of knowledge chooses a path with heart and follows it."

—Carlos Castaneda, *A Separate Reality*

It's time to get started, time to take action. Time to stop thinking about the old sole proprietorship and start thinking about the new business. It's not a matter of coming up with better businesses; it's about reinventing the business of home cleaning.

And the owner has to take personal responsibility for it.

That's you.

So sit up and pay attention!

You, the owner, have to be interested. You cannot abdicate accountability for the business of home cleaning, the administration of home cleaning, or the finance of home cleaning

Although the goal is to create systems into which an owner can plug reasonably competent people - systems that allow the business to run without them - owners must take responsibility for that happening.

I can hear the chorus now: "But we're just house cleaners! We shouldn't have to know about this." To that I say: *whatever*. If you don't give a flip about your business, fine - close your mind to new knowledge and accountability. But if you want to succeed, then you'd better step up and take responsibility, and you'd better do it now.

All too often, small business owners take no responsibility for the business of home cleaning but instead delegate tasks without any understanding of what it takes to do them; without any interest in what their people are actually doing; without any sense of what it feels like to be at the customer's home when a customer is kept waiting for a technician for four hours; and without any appreciation for the entity that is creating their livelihood.

These same owners can open the portals of change in an instant. All you have to do is say, "I don't want to do it that way anymore." Saying it will begin to set you free - even though you don't yet understand what the business will look like after it's been reinvented.

This demands an intentional leap from the known into the unknown. It further demands that you live there - in the unknown - for a while. It means discarding the past, everything you once believed to be true.

Think of it as soaring rather than plunging.

Thought Control

You should now be clear about the need to organize your thoughts first, then your business. Because the organization of your thoughts is the foundation for the organization of your business.

If we try to organize our business without organizing our thoughts, we will fail to attack the problem.

We have seen that organization is not simply time management. Nor is it people management. Nor is it tidying up desks or alphabetizing customer files. Organization is first, last, and always cleaning up the mess of our minds.

By learning how to *think* about the business of home cleaning, by learning how to *think* about your priorities, and by learning how to *think* about your life, you'll prepare yourself to do righteous battle with the forces of failure.

Right thinking leads to right action - and now is the time to take action. Because it is only through action that you can translate thoughts into movement in the real world, and, in the process, find fulfillmen

So, first, *think* about what you want to do. Then *do* it. Only in this way will you be fulfilled

How do you put the principles we've discussed in this book to work in your home cleaning business? To find out, accompany me down the path once more:

1. *Create a story about your company.* Your story should be an idealized version of your home cleaning company, a vision of what the pre-eminent example in your field should be and why. Your story must become the very heart of your business. It must become the spirit that mobilizes it, as well as everyone

who walks through the doors. Without this story, your business will be reduced to plain work.

2. *Organize your company so that it breathes life into your story.* Unless your company can faithfully replicate your story in action, it all becomes fiction. In that case, you'd be better off not telling your story at all. And without a story, you'd be better off leaving your business the way it is and just hoping for the best.

Here are some tips for organizing your home cleaning company:

- Identify the key functions of your business.
- Identify the essential processes that link those functions.
- Identify the results you have determined your company will produce.
- Clearly state in writing how each phase will work.

Take it step by step. Think of your business as a program, a piece of software, a *system*. It is a collaboration, a collection of processes dynamically interacting with one another.

Of course, your business is also people.

3. *Engage your people in the process.* Why is this the third step rather than the first? Because, contrary to the advice most business experts will give you, you must never engage your people in the process until you yourself are clear about what you intend to do.

The need for consensus is a disease of today's addled mind. It's a product of our troubled and confused times. When people don't know what to believe in, they often ask others to tell them. To ask is not to lead but to follow.

The prerequisite of sound leadership is first to know where you wish to go.

And so, "What do *I* want?" becomes the first question; not, "What do *they* want?" In your own business, the vision must first be yours. To follow another's vision is to abdicate your personal accountability, your leadership role, your true power.

In short, the role of leader cannot be delegated or shared. And without leadership, no home cleaning business will ever succeed.

Despite what you have been told, *win-win* is a secondary step, not a primary one. The opposite of *win-win* is not necessarily *they lose.*

Let's say "they" can win by choosing a good horse. The best choice will not be made by consensus. "Guys, what horse do you think we should ride?" will always lead to endless and worthless discussions. By the time you're done jawing, the horse will have already left the post.

Before you talk to your people about what you intend to do in your business and why you intend to do it, you need to reach an agreement with yourself.

It's important to know (1) *exactly* what you want, (2) how you intend to proceed, (3) what's important to you and what isn't, and (4) what you want the business to be and how you want it to get there.

Once you have that agreement, it's critical that you engage your people in a discussion about what you intend to do and why. Be clear - both with yourself and with them.

The Story

The story is paramount because it is your vision. Tell it with passion and conviction. Tell it with precision. Never hurry a great story. Unveil it slowly. Don't mumble or show embarrassment.

Never apologize or display false modesty. Look your audience in the eyes and tell your story as though it is the most important one they'll ever hear about business. *Your business.* The company into which you intend to pour your heart, your soul, your intelligence, your imagination, your time, your money, and your sweaty persistence.

Get into the storytelling zone. Behave as though it means everything to you. Show no equivocation when telling your story.

These tips are important because you're going to tell your story over and over - to customers, to new and old employees, to contractors, to subcontractors, to technicians, and to your family and friends. You're going to tell it at your church or synagogue, to your card-playing or fishing buddies, and to organizations such as Kiwanis, Rotary, YMCA, Hadassah, and Boy Scouts.

There are few moments in your life when telling a great story about a great company is inappropriate.

If it is to be persuasive, you must love your story. Do you think Walt Disney loved his Disneyland story? Or Ray Kroc his McDonald's story? What about Fred Smith at Federal Express? Or Debbi Fields at Mrs. Fields Cookies? Or Tom Watson Jr. at IBM?

Do you think these people loved their stories? Do you think others loved (and *still* love) to hear them? I daresay *all* successful entrepreneurs have loved the story of their business. Because that's what true entrepreneurs do. They tell stories that come to life in the form of their business.

Remember: A great story never fails. A great story is always a joy to hear.

In summary, you first need to clarify, both for yourself and for your people, the *story* of your business. Then you need to detail the *process* your business must go through to make your story become reality.

I call this the business development process. Others call it re-engineering, continuous improvement, reinventing your business, or total quality management.

Whatever you call it, you must take three distinct steps to succeed:

1. *Innovation.* Continue to find better ways of doin what you do.
2. *Quantificatio* . Once that is achieved, quantify the impact of these improvements on your business.
3. *Orchestration.* Once these improvements are verified orchestrate this better way of running your business so that it becomes your standard, to be repeated time and again.

In this way, the system works - no matter who's using it. And you've built a business that works consistently, predictably, systematically. A business you can depend on to operate exactly as promised, every single time.

Your vision, your people, your process - all linked.

A superior home cleaning business is a creation of your imagination, a product of your mind. So fire it up and get started! Now let's read what Russell has to say about *taking action.*

CHAPTER

26

Live the Dream

Russell O'Connell

"*Begin with the end in mind*"

—*Stephen Covey*

What do you want?

It seems to be a simple question, right? And, as far as your business is concerned, you might come up with an equally simple answer: "to make lots of money." But that mindset alone is probably not going to get you far. Rephrase the question a little, however, and something funny happens.

What do you want *from life*? What do you want to have experienced when your time here is over? The day that just passed will never come back—what do you want from the next?

What do you *need* to be happy?

These are all variants of the very same question, but framed like this, they suddenly get you thinking about what really means something to you. And that's the good stuff. That's what will drive you to accomplish great things.

Find *your* motivation. Forget what convention tells you about who you should be or what you should do. Don't let others dictate how you're going to live your life. There are so many "facts of life" that aren't really facts of life at all when you start thinking about them.

Take corporate careers, for instance. Many people stay in corporate jobs for decades, spending over a day per week on commuting and overtime. They have respectable professional titles, high salaries and find their jobs challenging in a good way—and that's where they keep their focus. And maybe that's right for them.

There *are* benefits to having a corporate career. You'll be part of something greater than yourself—maybe a movement that simply couldn't happen in a smaller company—and there's great peace of mind in knowing that you'll get your paycheck at the end of each month, for example.

But whatever it is that you choose to do for a living—you have to weigh in *all* the costs associated with your income. Commuting—both in terms of time and total transportation costs—and overtime are the most apparent, often bringing the actual hourly rate down significantl . And then there's the stress. Are you getting home late every workday, only having a few hours with your loved ones, exhausted from a long day at the offic and already thinking about what's on for tomorrow? What does that do to those precious moments that you have together? Are you truly present for each other? If not, what's it all for then!?

Not all careers are like that, of course. There are plenty of professionals who manage to go from strength to strength both in business and at home with their families. Hats off to all of you who do! We've all met them, perhaps envied them, too.

...But those lives are in the minority.

Maybe you consider yourself one of these people, and if so? I'm truly happy for you. But if you aren't—and at one time, I wasn't, either—there are lots of other options. Explore them--stretch yourself, dream, learn, ask, and in the end?

Choose what is truly "right."

The bottom line is this: don't just uncritically accept what life throws at you. Take ownership and act with intent. Be proactive instead of reactive.

And it's never too late to make new choices. It's your future. Shouldn't it be in your hands?

No one can tell you what you should do. It's your life. You have to decide. But if you can envision your dream life in detail, you've already begun the journey of a thousand steps. You know where you want to go. Now you just have to figure out how to get there. Step by step.

Keep the dream alive. As long as you do it with a purpose, you won't waste a second doing so. Dreaming is the domain of the pioneers, the visionaries, the entrepreneurs. It's how you *create* a life for yourself. And it's how you stay on course. Like in sailing, you'll have to tack against the wind sometimes, but as long as you begin and continue with the end in mind, pursuing it with passion, you'll be on the right track.

Now, let me introduce you to someone who has done exactly this. Josie. She's someone who didn't just create a new life for herself—she changed mine, too.

Josie had had a long corporate career in marketing when she got MyHome in to clean her family home. With an eye for branding, she looked beyond the satisfying results and saw a new future for herself.

At the time, I wasn't actually looking for partners. I had only recently returned to Australia from the UK, creating MyHome in Melbourne to have a business that worked *for* me and the life I wanted.

I was enjoying having the time to meet with customers and refine the MyHome systems. Knowing that our customers trusted us 100% and that we made a real difference in their busy lives felt great. But Josie showed me a deeper meaning to it all—something that I had been too busy to fully appreciate in the UK.

Josie came in to see me, explaining how impressed she was with our systems and wondering whether there could be an opportunity for us to do something together. She told me how she wanted a business of her own to grow and nurture. How she wanted more freedom and flexibility in her life. A four-day workweek and the ability to spend more time with her daughter and at her beach house, as well as volunteering for a local charity, The Sacred Heart Mission for the homeless.

What Josie saw in MyHome was a strong brand and a turnkey operating system, allowing her to apply herself and hit the ground running in pursuit of this dream of hers.

And what I saw in her was a driven, smart and compassionate person who was perfectly aligned with our values.

This is how the MyHome franchise started in Australia—through a shared passion for making every moment of our lives count.

Josie took ownership of a small territory around Albert Park, an affluen inner-city suburb internationally famous for hosting the annual Formula 1 Australian Grand Prix. Following MyHome's systems to the letter, she soon grew her business to the size she wanted it.

Today, Josie has a team of 6-8 staff and over a hundred customers, most of whom she knows personally. She starts her day briefing her teams over coffee at her favourite café. And with no need for an office she ll spend the rest of the workday wherever she likes. Then she wraps at around 4:00 p.m. or earlier to be with her family or help out at the Sacred Heart Mission.

Josie often takes long weekends at her beach house; she's got the peace of mind to care for herself and her loved ones; and she's got the money to do everything else that she enjoys doing. Important point: *this is her happy place.* Josie IS living HER dream. She doesn't *need* any more, so although she's got a long customer wait list, she keeps her business at the size it is.

No one tells this story better than Josie herself, though. You can hear it here:

Inspired by Josie, I proceeded in offering partnerships to other likeminded people. And let me tell you: it's made my life so much richer. Now MyHome isn't only making a difference to the lives of our customers and staff—we're an integral part of realizing the dreams of our partners. That means something far beyond money. It's about changing people's lives. It's about parents being able to be there for their children, about people helping others and becoming everything *they* want to be. It's ultimately about the most precious thing there is.

Time.

Life.

Now, in this book, Michael and I have outlined the steps that you *could* take to create the life that you want. Work methodically in creating your standards and systems, and you can predict your success with mathematical precision. The market for home-cleaning services is there for your taking. Put in the effort, and you *will* reap the rewards.

You can start right now. Take these five steps, and you will soon be miles ahead of the vast majority of home-cleaning businesses:

Answer the question, "why?"

Ask the question on two levels—for yourself and for your customers. You already know why your brand will exist for your customers, though: it's so that they can spend their time doing other things than cleaning. You'll be selling time to people whose time is worth a lot. But why are you doing this for yourself? What do you hope to achieve by building your business? What kind of life do you want? Answer this question truthfully. A strong why is your motivation for everything you'll be doing from this point. Take your time to imagine, in great detail, what your life will look like in five, ten and fifteen year

Answer the question, "what?"

What will you need to create your dream life? Exactly how much money will your goals require? What size business will you need to generate that kind of money? And what assets will you need to build such a business? Don't set your goals too high, nor too low. Your financial goals should be consistent with your dream life, or you won't find the drive to pursue them. Be precise

Answer the question, "how?"

Define your customers. Define your scope of services. Define your geographical footprint. Define your cleaning standards. Define, define, define! With exact definitions for as many business aspects as possible, you will find that the systems will present themselves. The need to stick to your definitions—your standards—will push you to identity the most efficien procedures for getting there.

Observe and document

Running everything strictly as per your established standards and systems, observe and document everything that goes on in your business. Without documentation, you'll be flying blind, never knowing whether you're on track or not. Notably, other than personal KPIs, etc., this requires understanding and monitoring of the four kinds of money. You should always know where your business is at in financial terms

Analyse, reevaluate and adjust

Look at the data. Are you and your team living up to each detailed standard? If not, is it due to human error or because the standard or system is untenable? And if you do meet all standards, is there an even more efficien way of doing it? This will bring you right back to the "what?" and "how?" questions as you work through each issue methodically—and for each completed cycle, your standards and procedures will improve.

That's the systems-based way of doing business. It turns the unknown into known, both in terms of definitions and mechanics, and from that point, you can calculate exactly what's going to happen next. You can be proactive instead of reactive, creating your own future.

In a way, it's not all too different from what you're doing right now. You already have multiple systems in place. It's just that you call them *habits*. And in business as in life, they will work for you—or against you. What sets entrepreneurs apart from technicians is that entrepreneurs know exactly what habits they have and how efficient they ar

So, start by making your habits visible to yourself.

Identify, standardize and systemize.

There's a new life waiting.

AFTERWORD

Michael E. Gerber

For more than four decades, I've applied The E-Myth principles I've shared with you in this book to the successful development of thousands of small businesses throughout the world. The industries represented have gone from one end of the spectrum to another, specializing in everything from landscaping to residential remodeling to commercial development to SaaS.

Few rewards are greater than seeing these E-Myth principles improve the work and lives of so many people. Those rewards include seeing these changes:

- Lack of clarity—clarifie
- Lack of organization—organized
- Lack of direction—shaped into a path that is clearly, lovingly, passionately pursued
- Lack of money or money poorly managed—money understood instead of coveted; created instead of chased; wisely spent or invested instead of squandered
- Lack of committed people—transformed into a cohesive community working in harmony toward a common goal; discovering each other and themselves in the process; all the while expanding their understanding, their know-how, their interest, their attention

After working with so many companies, I know that a business can be much more than what most become. I also know that nothing is preventing you from making your home cleaning business all that it can be. It takes only desire and the perseverance to see it through.

In this book—the next of its kind in The E-Myth Expert series—The E-Myth principles have been complemented and enriched by stories from Russell O'Connell, a real-life entrepreneur who has put these principles to use in his home cleaning enterprise. Russell had the desire and perseverance to achieve success beyond his wildest dreams. Now you, too, can join his ranks.

I hope this book has helped you clear your vision and set your sights on a very bright future.

To your business!

ABOUT THE AUTHORS

Michael E. Gerber

Michael E. Gerber is the world's #1 small business author of 32 books on entrepreneurship and small business management. His N.Y. Times bestseller, "The E-Myth Revisited: Why Most Small Businesses Don't Work And What to Do About It," is utilized in 118 universities as a foundational entrepre-neurial textbook, has been translated in 30 languages, and was utilized in the creation of the curriculum of Michael E. Gerber Companies™. Gerber aims to ***"bring the dream back to small business worldwide."*** Gerber has founded Radical U Trade School and Michael E. Gerber Partners™, which both aim to equip and inspire entrepreneurs at every stage of their journey. Mr. Gerber lives with his wife Luz Delia—who is the sole principal, partner, and CoFounder of Michael E. Gerber Companies™—in Houston, Texas.

Russell O'Connell

Russell O'Connell has an extraordinary story to tell. From humble beginnings starting his first business in his teens, to building one of the UK's largest franchise groups that's listed on the London Stock Exchange with £100 million market capitalization and operations in 9 countries. To get there, Russell was involved in numerous start-ups in diverse industries, including real estate, fashion, cosmetics and more. A restless disruptor, innovator, and systems man, Russell has a unique, innovative way of looking at business. He swears by the principle "Success is in the System™". His success sees him spending his time between Australia, Southeast Asia, and London. Russell has shared the stage with Tom Peters, Peter Drucker, and Stephen Covey, but is delighted to now share his story with the author that inspired him most, Michael E. Gerber.

TRANSFORMING THE STATE OF SMALL BUSINESS WORLDWIDE!

Yes—that's what we've been doing at **Michael E. Gerber Companies** for a generation of small-business startups and entrepreneurs.

Now **YOU** can accomplish that with us as well!

If you're a small-business owner, the founder of a new enterprise, or an entrepreneur creating your own kind of magic —in any industry or profession—we want to engage with you.

Because it all happens *one small business at a time.*
In stunning, original ways.
With no capital to speak of.
With no experience to speak of.
With simply the undying passion to create something that showed up in your mind—reminding you that magic is always a surprise, even to the Magician.

Yes, this is your moment, dear Reader.
This is the call you've been waiting for.

Become one of Michael E. Gerber's passionate CoAuthors.
Or ask to be Mentored by him.

But do it now—at this very moment.
Email us at: **gerber@michaelegerbercompanies.com**

ABOUT THE SERIES

The E-Myth Expert Series brings Michael E. Gerber's proven ***E-Myth*** philosophy to a wide range of professional practice areas. ***The E-Myth***—short for "The Entrepreneurial Myth"—is simple: Too many small businesses fail to grow because their leaders think like technicians instead of entrepreneurs. Gerber's approach provides small business leaders with practical, proven methods that have already transformed more than 70,000 businesses. Let ***The E-Myth*** Expert Series help you elevate your professional practice today!

Books in the Industry-Specific The E-Myth Expert Series include:

The E-Myth Accountant
The E-Myth Architect
The E-Myth Attorney
The E-Myth Bookkeeper
The E-Myth Chiropractor
The E-Myth Financial Advisor
The E-Myth Landscape Contractor
The E-Myth Real Estate Agent
The E-Myth Real Estate Brokerage
The E-Myth Real Estate Investor
The E-Myth Veterinarian
The E-Myth Chief Financial Officer
The E-Myth HVAC Contractor
The E-Myth Home Cleaning Business

Have you created an **E-Myth** enterprise? Would you like to become a CoAuthor of an **E-Myth** book in your industry?

Who do you know who is an expert in their industry?
Who has applied **E-Myth** to improve their practice as Russell O'Connell has in his Home Cleaning Business?
Who can add immense value to others in their industry by sharing what they've learned?

Please share this book with that individual—and share that individual with us. We at Michael E. Gerber Companies™ are determined to transform the state of small business and entrepreneurship worldwide.

JOIN THE E-MYTH EVOLUTION

Find the latest updates:

http://www.michaelegerbercompanies.com/

https://michaelegerbercompanies.com/coauthors/

Attend the Dreaming Room Trainings

www.michaelegerbercompanies.com/dreaming-room

Watch the latest videos

www.youtube.com/michaelegerber

Connect on LinkedIn

www.linkedin.com/in/michaelegerber

Connect on Facebook

www.facebook.com/MichaelEGerberCo/

Follow on X

https://x.com/MichaelEGerber

Connect with Russell O'Connell:

http://myhomeclean.com.au/

www.ingramcontent.com/pod-product-compliance
Lightning Source LLC
LaVergne TN
LVHW091514200926
848483LV00005B/417/J